ENTREPRENEURSHIP

FROM DREAM TO REALITY

SAGAR SHINDE

ENTREPRENEURSHIP

From dream to reality

SAGAR SHINDE

Table of Contents

Introduction

Part I: Preparing for Entrepreneurship

Part II: Launching Your Business

Part III: Growing Your Business

Introduction

Introduction

Welcome to "Entrepreneurship 101: From Dream to Reality." This book is designed to be your comprehensive guide to the world of entrepreneurship, providing you with the knowledge and tools necessary to transform your entrepreneurial dreams into a thriving reality. Whether you are just starting out or looking to take your existing business to the next level, this book will equip you with the essential principles, strategies, and practical advice needed to navigate the challenges and opportunities that come with entrepreneurship.

In this introduction, we will explore the essence of entrepreneurship and the mindset required for success. We will delve into the characteristics of successful entrepreneurs and help you cultivate the entrepreneurial mindset that will drive your journey forward.

Chapter 1, "The Entrepreneurial Mindset," begins by defining entrepreneurship and highlighting its significance in today's rapidly evolving business landscape. We will explore the key traits and qualities that distinguish successful entrepreneurs, such as passion, resilience, creativity, and a willingness to take calculated risks. By understanding these characteristics, you will gain insights into what it takes to succeed as an entrepreneur.

Furthermore, in Chapter 1, we will delve into the process of developing an entrepreneurial mindset. You will learn how to cultivate a growth mindset that embraces challenges, embraces failure as a learning opportunity, and fosters an attitude of continuous improvement. We will explore various techniques and strategies to develop an entrepreneurial mindset that will empower you to navigate the uncertainties and complexities of the entrepreneurial journey.

Throughout this book, we will take a step-by-step approach, guiding you through the various stages of entrepreneurship, from identifying opportunities and creating a solid business plan to launching your venture, building a strong team, and sustaining long-term success. Each chapter will provide practical insights, real-world examples, and actionable steps to help you apply the concepts discussed to your own entrepreneurial endeavors.

It's important to note that entrepreneurship is not a one-size-fits-all journey. Every entrepreneur's path is unique, and there are no guarantees of success. However, by arming yourself with knowledge, adopting an entrepreneurial mindset, and utilizing the strategies and principles outlined in this book, you will significantly increase your chances of turning your dreams into a thriving reality.

So, whether you're an aspiring entrepreneur seeking to take that first leap or an experienced business owner looking for fresh insights and strategies, "Entrepreneurship 101: From Dream to Reality" will serve as your trusted companion throughout your entrepreneurial journey. Let's embark on this exciting adventure together and unlock your full entrepreneurial potential!

Chapter 1
The Entrepreneurial Mindset

Introduction to the Entrepreneurial Mindset

Welcome to the chapter on the entrepreneurial mindset, a crucial aspect of becoming a successful entrepreneur. In this chapter, we will explore the fundamental principles and attitudes that shape the mindset of entrepreneurs and set them apart from others. Developing an entrepreneurial mindset is not only essential for starting and growing a business, but it also plays a significant role in personal growth and professional success.

Entrepreneurship is not just about starting a business; it is a way of thinking, problem-solving, and approaching opportunities and challenges. It requires a unique set of attitudes and beliefs that enable individuals to navigate the uncertain and ever-changing landscape of the business world.

In this chapter, we will begin by defining what the entrepreneurial mindset is and why it matters. We will explore the key characteristics and qualities that successful entrepreneurs possess and discuss how these traits contribute to their achievements. By understanding these attributes, you will gain insights into the mindset necessary for entrepreneurial success.

Next, we will delve into the process of developing an entrepreneurial mindset. We will explore techniques and strategies that can help you cultivate the mindset required to identify opportunities, take calculated risks, and persevere through challenges. By adopting an entrepreneurial mindset, you will be better equipped to embrace uncertainty, learn from failures, and continuously innovate.

Throughout this chapter, we will share inspiring stories of renowned entrepreneurs who have demonstrated exceptional entrepreneurial mindsets. Their experiences will provide valuable insights and practical examples of how the entrepreneurial mindset can drive success.

It's important to note that developing an entrepreneurial mindset is a journey that requires continuous learning and self-reflection. By the end of this chapter, you will have a solid foundation to begin cultivating your entrepreneurial mindset and integrate it into your personal and professional life.

So, whether you are an aspiring entrepreneur embarking on your first venture or an experienced entrepreneur seeking to refine your mindset, this chapter will provide you with the necessary knowledge and tools to foster an entrepreneurial mindset. Get ready to unlock your full potential and embrace the mindset that will propel you towards entrepreneurial success.

1.1 Defining Entrepreneurship

Entrepreneurship is a dynamic and multifaceted concept that encompasses a range of activities and mindsets. It involves the identification, creation, and pursuit of opportunities to bring about innovation and change. At its core, entrepreneurship is about taking risks, creating value, and making a meaningful impact on society.

Defining entrepreneurship can be challenging because it goes beyond the traditional notion of starting and running a business. While entrepreneurship often involves launching new ventures, it also extends to activities within existing organizations, such as intrapreneurship, where individuals drive innovation and growth from within.

Entrepreneurs are individuals who possess the vision, passion, and determination to transform ideas into reality. They are willing to take calculated risks, embrace uncertainty, and work tirelessly to bring about positive change. Entrepreneurs have a unique ability to identify opportunities in the market, develop innovative solutions, and create value for customers and stakeholders.

Entrepreneurship is not limited to a particular industry or sector. It can manifest in various forms, such as social entrepreneurship, which focuses on addressing social or environmental challenges, or tech entrepreneurship, which involves leveraging technology to disrupt and revolutionize industries. Regardless of the specific context, entrepreneurship is characterized by a mindset of resilience, adaptability, and a relentless pursuit of growth and impact.

Moreover, entrepreneurship is not solely about financial success or personal gain. It encompasses a broader vision of creating sustainable businesses that generate value for all stakeholders, including employees, customers, communities, and the environment. Entrepreneurs often strive to make a positive difference in the world by tackling societal problems, fostering innovation, and driving economic development.

In summary, entrepreneurship is a multifaceted concept that involves identifying opportunities, taking risks, and creating value. It is driven by individuals with a unique mindset and a passion for making a meaningful impact. Whether it involves starting a new business, introducing innovation within an organization, or pursuing a social cause, entrepreneurship is a powerful force that fuels economic growth, societal progress, and personal fulfillment.

1.2 Characteristics of Successful Entrepreneurs

Successful entrepreneurs possess a distinct set of characteristics that contribute to their achievements and differentiate them from others. While every entrepreneur is unique, there are several common traits that consistently appear among those who have achieved significant success. Understanding these characteristics can provide valuable insights and guidance for aspiring entrepreneurs. Let's explore some key traits of successful entrepreneurs:

1. Passion and Persistence: Successful entrepreneurs are driven by a deep passion for what they do. They have a genuine enthusiasm for their business and a strong belief in their vision. This passion fuels their persistence, enabling them to overcome challenges, persevere through setbacks, and maintain focus on their goals.

2. Risk-Taking and Resilience: Entrepreneurship inherently involves taking risks, and successful entrepreneurs are willing to embrace and manage them. They have the courage to step out of their comfort zones, make bold decisions, and face uncertainty head-on. Additionally, they demonstrate resilience, bouncing back from failures, learning from setbacks, and using them as opportunities for growth.

3. Visionary Thinking: Successful entrepreneurs possess a visionary mindset. They can see beyond the present and envision possibilities for the future. They have the ability to identify emerging trends, anticipate market needs, and innovate accordingly. Their vision guides their strategic planning, decision-making, and overall direction for their businesses.

4. Adaptability and Flexibility: Entrepreneurship requires the ability to adapt to changing circumstances and embrace flexibility. Successful entrepreneurs are open to new ideas, willing to pivot when necessary,

and agile in responding to market dynamics. They can navigate through uncertainty and adjust their strategies to stay relevant and seize opportunities.

5. Continuous Learning and Curiosity: Entrepreneurs have a thirst for knowledge and a commitment to lifelong learning. They seek out new information, stay updated on industry trends, and actively seek feedback. Successful entrepreneurs are curious and constantly strive to expand their knowledge, skills, and perspectives.

6. Strong Work Ethic and Self-Discipline: Entrepreneurship demands hard work and dedication. Successful entrepreneurs possess a strong work ethic, often going above and beyond what is expected. They have the self-discipline to stay focused, set priorities, and manage their time effectively. They understand that success requires consistent effort and are willing to put in the necessary work.

7. Effective Communication and Leadership: Entrepreneurs need to communicate their vision, build relationships, and inspire others. Successful entrepreneurs are effective communicators, both in conveying their ideas and listening to feedback. They possess leadership skills that allow them to motivate and empower their teams, foster collaboration, and drive collective efforts towards a shared goal.

8. Resourcefulness and Problem-Solving: Entrepreneurs often face resource constraints and encounter complex problems. Successful entrepreneurs are resourceful, finding creative ways to overcome limitations and leverage available resources effectively. They have strong problem-solving skills, approaching challenges with a solution-oriented mindset and embracing innovation to find unique solutions.

While these characteristics are not exhaustive, they provide valuable insights into the mindset and qualities of successful entrepreneurs.

It's important to note that these traits can be developed and honed over time through self-reflection, continuous learning, and practical experience. By cultivating these characteristics, aspiring entrepreneurs can increase their chances of success and navigate the entrepreneurial journey with confidence.

1.3 Developing an Entrepreneurial Mindset

Developing an entrepreneurial mindset is crucial for aspiring entrepreneurs who aim to turn their dreams into a thriving reality. It involves adopting a specific set of attitudes, beliefs, and behaviors that empower individuals to navigate the challenges, seize opportunities, and drive their entrepreneurial ventures forward. While some people may naturally possess certain entrepreneurial traits, developing an entrepreneurial mindset is a continuous process that can be nurtured and enhanced. Here are some key steps to cultivate an entrepreneurial mindset:

1. Embrace a Growth Mindset: A growth mindset is the belief that intelligence and abilities can be developed through dedication, hard work, and continuous learning. Embracing a growth mindset allows you to view challenges as opportunities for growth, learn from failures, and persist in the face of setbacks. Recognize that your skills and abilities are not fixed but can be improved with effort and practice.

2. Cultivate a Bias for Action: Successful entrepreneurs are not afraid to take action and make decisions, even in the face of uncertainty. Develop a bias for action by embracing calculated risk-taking and overcoming analysis paralysis. Start small, test ideas, and iterate based on feedback and results. Taking action is crucial for progress and learning.

3. Foster Creativity and Innovation: Entrepreneurs thrive on creativity and innovation. Cultivate a mindset that encourages thinking outside the box, challenging assumptions, and exploring new possibilities. Embrace curiosity and seek diverse perspectives to spark fresh ideas and approaches. Look for opportunities to innovate and differentiate yourself in the market.

4. Embrace Failure as a Learning Opportunity: Failure is an inevitable part of entrepreneurship, but successful entrepreneurs view it as a valuable learning experience. Embrace failure as an opportunity for growth, resilience, and learning. Analyze your failures, extract lessons from them, and apply those insights to future endeavors. See failure not as a setback but as a stepping stone toward success.

5. Develop a Strong Network: Surround yourself with like-minded individuals who share your entrepreneurial spirit. Build a network of mentors, peers, and experts who can provide guidance, support, and inspiration. Engage in communities, attend industry events, and seek out mentors who can offer insights and valuable connections.

6. Nurture a Proactive and Problem-Solving Attitude: Entrepreneurs are proactive and solution-oriented. Cultivate a mindset that sees problems as opportunities for innovation and creative problem-solving. Develop the ability to identify challenges, break them down into manageable tasks, and find effective solutions. Embrace resilience and persevere in the face of obstacles.

7. Continuously Learn and Seek Feedback: Commit to lifelong learning and seek opportunities to expand your knowledge and skills. Stay updated on industry trends, emerging technologies, and market dynamics. Actively seek feedback from customers, mentors, and peers to gain insights and improve your offerings. Be open to constructive criticism and use it as a catalyst for growth.

Remember, developing an entrepreneurial mindset is an ongoing journey that requires self-reflection, determination, and a commitment to personal and professional growth. By cultivating these qualities and adopting an entrepreneurial mindset, you will be better equipped to seize opportunities, overcome challenges, and navigate the entrepreneurial landscape with confidence and resilience.

Part I:
Preparing for Entrepreneurship

Chapter 2
Identifying Opportunities

Introduction

Welcome to the chapter on identifying opportunities, a critical aspect of entrepreneurship. In this chapter, we will explore the process of recognizing and evaluating opportunities that have the potential to be transformed into successful ventures. Identifying opportunities is the first step towards turning your entrepreneurial dreams into reality. By understanding how to spot opportunities and assess their viability, you can set yourself on a path towards entrepreneurial success.

In this chapter, we will begin by discussing the importance of identifying opportunities in the entrepreneurial journey. We will explore why opportunity recognition is a key driver of innovation, growth, and competitive advantage. Understanding the significance of identifying opportunities will inspire you to actively seek out and capitalize on emerging possibilities.

Next, we will delve into the various sources of entrepreneurial opportunities. Opportunities can arise from changes in the market, technological advancements, social trends, or personal experiences. By exploring these different sources, you will expand your perspective and enhance your ability to identify opportunities in diverse contexts.

Furthermore, we will explore the process of opportunity recognition. We will discuss the mindset and skills necessary to spot opportunities, including being observant, curious, and open to new ideas. You will learn how to analyze market trends, conduct market research, and identify unmet needs or gaps in the market that can serve as potential opportunities.

In this chapter, we will also delve into the evaluation of opportunities. Identifying an opportunity is just the first step; you need to assess its feasibility, viability, and potential for success. We will explore techniques such as market analysis, competitive analysis, and financial analysis to help you evaluate the potential of an opportunity and make informed decisions.

Throughout this chapter, we will share real-world examples of successful entrepreneurs who identified and capitalized on opportunities. Their stories will provide valuable insights into the mindset and strategies that contribute to successful opportunity recognition.

It's important to note that identifying opportunities is not a one-time event but an ongoing process. The entrepreneurial landscape is constantly evolving, presenting new challenges and possibilities. By honing your skills in identifying opportunities, you can stay ahead of the curve and position yourself for entrepreneurial success.

So, whether you are an aspiring entrepreneur seeking your first venture or an experienced entrepreneur looking to expand your portfolio, this chapter will equip you with the knowledge and tools to identify and evaluate opportunities effectively. Get ready to sharpen your entrepreneurial vision and embark on the journey of identifying opportunities that can shape your entrepreneurial future.

2.1 Recognizing Market Gaps and Trends

Recognizing market gaps and trends is a crucial aspect of identifying entrepreneurial opportunities. By understanding the needs and preferences of consumers, as well as the dynamics of the market, entrepreneurs can identify unmet needs and emerging trends that can serve as potential opportunities for innovative solutions and business ventures. In this section, we will explore the process of recognizing market gaps and trends to uncover opportunities for entrepreneurial success.

1. Understanding Consumer Needs: One of the key steps in recognizing market gaps is gaining a deep understanding of consumer needs and pain points. By listening to customers, conducting market research, and analyzing consumer behavior, entrepreneurs can identify areas where existing products or services fail to meet consumer demands or where there are untapped opportunities for improvement.

2. Conducting Market Research: Market research plays a vital role in recognizing market gaps and trends. It involves collecting and analyzing data related to the market, competitors, and target customers. Through market research, entrepreneurs can identify underserved segments, changing customer preferences, and emerging trends that can inform the development of innovative solutions.

3. Observing Industry and Market Trends: Staying abreast of industry and market trends is essential for recognizing opportunities. By monitoring trends, entrepreneurs can identify shifts in consumer behavior, technological advancements, regulatory changes, and emerging market niches. Keeping a finger on the pulse of the market allows entrepreneurs to identify gaps that can be filled with innovative products, services, or business models.

4. Identifying Pain Points and Frictions: Opportunities often arise from identifying pain points and frictions in existing products, services, or processes. By recognizing areas where customers experience difficulties, inefficiencies, or dissatisfaction, entrepreneurs can develop solutions that address these pain points and provide a superior customer experience.

5. Analyzing Competitive Landscape: Analyzing the competitive landscape helps entrepreneurs identify gaps where competitors are underserving customers or where there is limited competition. By understanding the strengths and weaknesses of existing players, entrepreneurs can position themselves strategically to fill gaps and offer unique value propositions.

6. Embracing Technological Advancements: Technological advancements can create new market opportunities and disrupt existing industries. By staying informed about emerging technologies and their potential applications, entrepreneurs can identify opportunities to leverage technology to solve problems, enhance efficiency, or create new customer experiences.

7. Recognizing Social and Cultural Shifts: Changes in society, culture, and demographics often lead to new market opportunities. Entrepreneurs who are attuned to these shifts can identify emerging needs, changing consumer preferences, and untapped markets. By recognizing and catering to these evolving trends, entrepreneurs can position themselves ahead of the curve.

Remember, recognizing market gaps and trends requires a combination of research, observation, and intuition. It involves staying curious, being proactive in gathering information, and continuously monitoring the business environment. By honing your ability to identify market gaps and trends, you can uncover opportunities that have the potential to drive entrepreneurial success.

2.2 Conducting Market Research

Market research is a crucial step in identifying and evaluating entrepreneurial opportunities. It involves gathering and analyzing data about the market, target customers, competitors, and industry trends. By conducting comprehensive market research, entrepreneurs can gain valuable insights that inform their decision-making and increase their chances of success. In this section, we will explore the process of conducting market research and its significance in identifying entrepreneurial opportunities.

1. Define Your Research Objectives: Before conducting market research, it is essential to define clear research objectives. What specific information do you need to gather? What questions do you want to answer? Defining your research objectives will help you focus your efforts and ensure that the data you collect is relevant to your entrepreneurial venture.

2. Identify Your Target Market: Determine the specific segment of the market that you intend to serve. Understanding your target market allows you to tailor your research efforts to gather insights specific to that audience. Consider demographics, psychographics, geographic location, and other relevant factors that define your target market.

3. Select Appropriate Research Methods: There are various research methods that you can employ to gather market data. Common methods include surveys, interviews, focus groups, observation, and secondary research. Choose the methods that are most suitable for your research objectives, budget, and time constraints.

4. Conduct Primary Research: Primary research involves gathering data directly from your target market or other relevant sources. This could include conducting surveys or interviews with potential customers, industry experts, or key stakeholders. Primary research

provides firsthand insights into customer needs, preferences, and behaviors.

5. **Utilize Secondary Research:** Secondary research involves gathering data from existing sources such as industry reports, market studies, academic publications, and government statistics. Secondary research provides valuable background information, industry trends, and competitor analysis. It can help you understand the broader market landscape and identify existing gaps or opportunities.

6. **Analyze and Interpret Data:** Once you have collected the necessary data, analyze and interpret the findings. Look for patterns, trends, and insights that can inform your decision-making. Use tools and techniques such as data visualization, statistical analysis, and qualitative coding to gain a deeper understanding of the data.

7. **Stay Updated:** Market research is an ongoing process, and it is crucial to stay updated on the latest market trends and changes. Continuously monitor the market, industry news, competitor activities, and customer feedback to stay informed and adapt your strategies accordingly.

8. **Validate Findings:** It is essential to validate your research findings to ensure their accuracy and reliability. Consider seeking external validation through expert opinions, peer reviews, or pilot studies. Validating your findings helps build confidence in your research and the decisions you make based on it.

Remember, market research provides valuable insights that guide your entrepreneurial journey. It helps you understand your target market, identify customer needs, evaluate market dynamics, and assess the viability of your business ideas. By investing time and effort into conducting comprehensive market research, you can make informed decisions and increase your chances of success in identifying and capitalizing on entrepreneurial opportunities.

2.3 Assessing Personal Interests and Skills

Assessing your personal interests and skills is a critical step in identifying entrepreneurial opportunities that align with your strengths and passions. By understanding your unique abilities and areas of interest, you can identify opportunities that resonate with you and increase your chances of success. In this section, we will explore the process of assessing personal interests and skills and how they contribute to entrepreneurial success.

1. Reflect on Your Interests: Start by reflecting on your personal interests and passions. What are you genuinely enthusiastic about? What topics, industries, or activities energize you? Identifying your interests will help you find opportunities that align with your passion and motivation, increasing your chances of enjoying and excelling in your entrepreneurial journey.

2. Identify Your Skills and Expertise: Assess your skills and expertise across different domains. What are you naturally good at? What knowledge and experience do you possess? Identify your strengths, whether they are technical skills, creative abilities, leadership qualities, or problem-solving capabilities. Understanding your skills will help you leverage them effectively in entrepreneurial opportunities.

3. Consider Transferable Skills: Transferable skills are those that can be applied across various industries or roles. Evaluate your transferable skills, such as communication, adaptability, project management, or critical thinking. These skills can be valuable assets in entrepreneurial ventures, allowing you to navigate different challenges and seize opportunities.

4. Assess Your Risk Tolerance: Entrepreneurship often involves taking risks and stepping outside your comfort zone. Assess your

risk tolerance and willingness to embrace uncertainty. Are you comfortable with ambiguity and making decisions in uncertain situations? Evaluating your risk tolerance will help you gauge your readiness for entrepreneurial opportunities that may involve calculated risks.

5. Seek Feedback: Seek feedback from trusted mentors, advisors, or peers who can provide an objective perspective on your interests and skills. They can help you identify strengths you may overlook and provide insights on areas where you can further develop your capabilities. Feedback from others can provide valuable guidance in recognizing entrepreneurial opportunities that align with your abilities.

6. Identify Skill Gaps: Identify areas where you may have skill gaps or areas for improvement. Consider whether acquiring additional knowledge or skills would enhance your entrepreneurial capabilities. Determine if you need to invest in learning or seek partnerships or collaborations to complement your skill set.

7. Find the Intersection: Look for the intersection between your interests, skills, and entrepreneurial opportunities. Identify areas where your passions align with market needs or where your skills can provide a competitive advantage. The sweet spot between your personal strengths and market demand is where you are more likely to find success and fulfillment as an entrepreneur.

8. Continuously Develop Yourself: Entrepreneurship is a continuous learning journey. Commit to personal and professional development by seeking opportunities to enhance your skills, expand your knowledge, and refine your areas of interest. Stay updated on industry trends and emerging technologies to remain relevant in your chosen field.

By assessing your personal interests and skills, you can align your entrepreneurial endeavors with your passions and strengths. This alignment increases your motivation, resilience, and overall satisfaction in pursuing entrepreneurial opportunities. Remember, self-awareness and ongoing self-assessment are essential in recognizing opportunities that are not only financially rewarding but also personally fulfilling.

Chapter 3
Creating a Business Plan

Introduction

Congratulations on identifying an entrepreneurial opportunity! Now it's time to transform your idea into a comprehensive plan of action. In this chapter, we will guide you through the process of creating a business plan, a crucial document that outlines your business concept, strategies, and financial projections. A well-crafted business plan serves as a roadmap to guide your entrepreneurial journey and communicate your vision to potential investors, partners, and stakeholders.

This chapter will take you through the essential elements of a business plan and provide you with the necessary tools and frameworks to develop a comprehensive and effective document. From the executive summary to the financial projections, you will learn how to present your business concept in a compelling and strategic manner.

Throughout the chapter, we will emphasize the importance of a business plan as a strategic tool for clarifying your vision, identifying potential challenges, and assessing the viability of your venture. It will help you analyze market dynamics, define your target market, articulate your value proposition, and outline your marketing and operational strategies.

The chapter will cover the following key areas:

1. Executive Summary: The executive summary is a concise overview of your business plan that captures the essence of your venture. It provides an introduction to your business concept, highlights the market opportunity, outlines your competitive advantage, and summarizes your financial projections. The executive summary serves as a hook to grab the attention of readers and entice them to delve deeper into your business plan.

2. Business Description: In this section, you will provide a detailed description of your business, including its mission, vision, and core values. You will articulate your unique value proposition, explain how your product or service addresses customer needs, and highlight your competitive advantage. This section sets the stage for the rest of your business plan.

3. Market Analysis: The market analysis section involves researching and analyzing the target market, industry trends, customer demographics, and competitors. You will demonstrate your understanding of the market landscape, identify your target customers, assess market size and growth potential, and evaluate the competitive landscape. This analysis will help you position your business strategically within the market.

4. Marketing and Sales Strategy: Here, you will outline your marketing and sales strategies to attract and retain customers. You will define your target market segments, discuss your pricing strategy, promotional activities, distribution channels, and customer acquisition and retention plans. Your marketing and sales strategies should align with your overall business objectives and value proposition.

5. Operational Plan: The operational plan details how your business will function on a day-to-day basis. It covers aspects such as your

organizational structure, key personnel, production or service delivery processes, and quality control measures. This section demonstrates your ability to execute your business concept effectively.

6. **Financial Projections:** Financial projections are a critical component of your business plan, providing a forecast of your expected revenue, expenses, and profitability over a specified period. You will outline your startup costs, projected sales, cash flow projections, and break-even analysis. Financial projections help assess the financial feasibility and sustainability of your venture.

7. **Risk Assessment and Mitigation:** Identifying and addressing potential risks is crucial for the success of your business. In this section, you will assess the risks and challenges that your venture may face and develop strategies to mitigate them. It shows that you have thought through the potential obstacles and have contingency plans in place.

By the end of this chapter, you will have a comprehensive understanding of the components that make up a business plan and how to craft a compelling document that effectively communicates your business concept, strategies, and financial projections. A well-developed business plan will not only serve as a roadmap for your entrepreneurial journey but also enhance your credibility with investors and stakeholders. Get ready to transform your entrepreneurial opportunity into a well-structured plan that sets the foundation for your business's success.

3.1 Components of a Business Plan

A business plan is a comprehensive document that outlines your business concept, strategies, and financial projections. It serves as a roadmap to guide your entrepreneurial journey and communicates your vision to potential investors, partners, and stakeholders. In this section, we will explore the essential components of a business plan and their significance in presenting a clear and compelling case for your venture.

1. Executive Summary: The executive summary is a concise overview of your business plan, typically written after completing the rest of the document. It provides a snapshot of your business concept, market opportunity, competitive advantage, and financial projections. The executive summary serves as a hook to grab the attention of readers and entice them to delve deeper into your business plan.

2. Business Description: The business description section provides a detailed overview of your business, including its mission, vision, and core values. It articulates your unique value proposition, explaining how your product or service addresses customer needs. This section highlights your competitive advantage and defines your business's identity and purpose.

3. Market Analysis: The market analysis section demonstrates your understanding of the target market, industry trends, customer demographics, and competitors. It includes market research findings, such as market size, growth potential, and customer behavior. This section helps you identify your target customers, assess market dynamics, and evaluate the competitive landscape. It also highlights the market gaps or opportunities that your business can capitalize on.

4. Marketing and Sales Strategy: The marketing and sales strategy outlines how you will attract and retain customers. It defines your

target market segments and discusses your pricing strategy, promotional activities, distribution channels, and customer acquisition and retention plans. This section demonstrates your ability to position your product or service effectively within the market and create a compelling marketing and sales approach.

5. Operational Plan: The operational plan details how your business will function on a day-to-day basis. It covers aspects such as your organizational structure, key personnel, production or service delivery processes, and quality control measures. This section demonstrates your ability to execute your business concept effectively and efficiently.

6. Financial Projections: Financial projections provide a forecast of your expected revenue, expenses, and profitability over a specified period. It includes a detailed analysis of your startup costs, projected sales, cash flow projections, and break-even analysis. This section helps assess the financial feasibility and sustainability of your venture. It also provides crucial information for investors and lenders to evaluate the potential return on investment and risk associated with funding your business.

7. Risk Assessment and Mitigation: The risk assessment and mitigation section identifies and addresses potential risks and challenges that your venture may face. It includes an analysis of market risks, operational risks, financial risks, and any other relevant risks specific to your industry or business model. This section demonstrates your ability to identify potential obstacles and develop strategies to mitigate them, ensuring the long-term success of your business.

8. Appendix: The appendix is an optional section where you can include additional supporting documents, such as market research reports, resumes of key team members, product/service brochures, or

any other relevant materials. Including an appendix allows readers to delve deeper into specific aspects of your business plan, if desired.

Each component of the business plan plays a crucial role in presenting a comprehensive and strategic case for your venture. By addressing these components thoughtfully and thoroughly, you will create a document that effectively communicates your business concept, strategies, and financial projections, setting a strong foundation for your entrepreneurial success.

3.2 Defining Your Value Proposition

The value proposition is a crucial element of your business plan that communicates the unique value and benefits your product or service offers to customers. It differentiates your business from competitors and convinces customers why they should choose your offering. In this section, we will explore how to define and articulate your value proposition effectively.

1. Understand Customer Needs: To define a compelling value proposition, you must have a deep understanding of your target customers' needs, pain points, and desires. Conduct market research, surveys, and interviews to gather insights into what motivates your customers and what they are looking for in a solution. Understanding their needs will help you align your value proposition with their expectations.

2. Identify Differentiating Factors: Analyze your product or service and identify what sets it apart from competitors. Consider its unique features, attributes, or benefits that deliver value to customers. These differentiating factors can be tangible, such as innovative technology or superior quality, or intangible, such as exceptional customer

service or a seamless user experience. Highlighting these factors will make your value proposition stand out in the market.

3. Focus on Customer Benefits: Your value proposition should clearly communicate the benefits customers will experience by using your product or service. How does it solve their problems, meet their needs, or fulfill their desires? Emphasize the outcomes, cost savings, convenience, time savings, or emotional satisfaction that customers will gain. Frame your value proposition in terms of the value customers receive, rather than simply describing product features.

4. Communicate Unique Selling Points: Identify the key selling points that make your offering unique and compelling. These can include factors such as price, quality, functionality, performance, convenience, customization options, or sustainability. Highlight these unique selling points in your value proposition to differentiate your business from competitors and capture customers' attention.

5. Keep It Clear and Concise: A strong value proposition is clear, concise, and easily understood by customers. Avoid using technical jargon or industry-specific terms that may confuse or alienate your target audience. Use simple language and convey your value proposition in a way that resonates with your customers' needs and preferences.

6. Test and Refine: Once you have developed a value proposition, test it with your target audience. Seek feedback, conduct surveys, or perform focus groups to understand how well your value proposition resonates with customers. Based on the feedback received, refine and iterate your value proposition to make it even more compelling and aligned with customer expectations.

7. Incorporate into Marketing and Communication: Your value proposition should be integrated into your marketing and communication efforts across various channels. Use it in your

website copy, social media posts, advertising campaigns, and sales pitches. Consistently communicate your value proposition to reinforce your unique position in the market and attract customers who resonate with your offering.

Remember, a strong value proposition is a key differentiator in the marketplace. It communicates the unique value your business offers and why customers should choose you over competitors. By defining and articulating your value proposition effectively, you can capture the attention and loyalty of your target audience, setting a strong foundation for the success of your entrepreneurial venture.

3.3 Crafting a Competitive Analysis

A competitive analysis is an essential component of your business plan that examines the strengths and weaknesses of your competitors in the marketplace. It provides valuable insights into their strategies, products or services, target customers, pricing, and positioning. Conducting a thorough competitive analysis allows you to identify opportunities, differentiate your business, and develop effective strategies to gain a competitive edge. In this section, we will explore the steps involved in crafting a comprehensive competitive analysis.

1. Identify Competitors: Begin by identifying your direct and indirect competitors in the market. Direct competitors offer similar products or services, target the same customer segment, and operate in the same geographic area. Indirect competitors may have different offerings but still serve the same customer needs or compete for the same market share. Make a list of both types of competitors to ensure a comprehensive analysis.

2. Research Competitor Strategies: Analyze the strategies employed by your competitors. This includes their pricing strategies, marketing and advertising tactics, distribution channels, product or service differentiation, customer service approaches, and any unique selling propositions. Look for patterns or trends that can provide insights into their competitive advantage or areas where they may be vulnerable.

3. Assess Strengths and Weaknesses: Evaluate the strengths and weaknesses of each competitor. Consider factors such as their brand reputation, customer loyalty, financial resources, product quality, customer service, market share, and any other relevant aspects. Identify areas where your competitors excel and where they may have limitations or gaps. This analysis will help you understand how your business can differentiate and position itself effectively.

4. Analyze Customer Perception: Understand how customers perceive your competitors. This can be done through customer surveys, reviews, social media monitoring, or analyzing industry reports. Gain insights into what customers appreciate about your competitors and where they may be dissatisfied. This information will guide you in developing strategies to meet customer needs better or offer unique value that sets you apart.

5. Identify Market Opportunities: As you analyze your competitors, look for untapped market opportunities or areas where customer needs are not fully addressed. This could be in the form of underserved customer segments, unmet needs, or gaps in the market that your business can capitalize on. By identifying these opportunities, you can develop strategies to position your business as a solution provider in those areas.

6. Differentiate Your Business: Based on your competitive analysis, identify how your business can differentiate itself from competitors. Determine what unique value or benefits you can offer to customers that your competitors don't. This could be through product innovation, superior customer service, pricing strategies, partnerships, or other creative approaches. Highlight these differentiating factors in your business plan to showcase your competitive advantage.

7. Develop Competitive Strategies: Use the insights gained from your competitive analysis to develop effective strategies that leverage your strengths and exploit your competitors' weaknesses. This may involve adjusting your pricing, enhancing your product or service offerings, improving customer service, targeting specific customer segments, or pursuing innovative marketing tactics. Your competitive strategies should align with your overall business objectives and value proposition.

8. Continuously Monitor the Competition: A competitive analysis is an ongoing process. Stay updated on changes in the market, new entrants, shifts in customer preferences, and evolving industry trends. Regularly revisit and refine your competitive analysis to adapt your strategies as needed.

Crafting a comprehensive competitive analysis is essential for understanding the competitive landscape and developing effective strategies to differentiate your business. By identifying opportunities, assessing your competitors' strengths and weaknesses, and leveraging your own competitive advantage, you can position your business for success in the marketplace.

3.4 Financial Projections and Budgeting

Financial projections and budgeting are critical components of your business plan that provide a comprehensive overview of your venture's financial outlook. They help you assess the financial feasibility of your business, plan for future growth, and demonstrate the potential return on investment to investors and stakeholders. In this section, we will explore the steps involved in creating financial projections and developing a budget for your business.

1. Revenue Projections: Start by estimating your revenue projections. This involves forecasting the sales volume of your products or services over a specific period, typically broken down by month, quarter, or year. Consider factors such as market demand, pricing strategy, marketing efforts, and competition when making revenue projections. Ensure that your projections are realistic and based on thorough market research and analysis.

2. Cost of Goods Sold (COGS): Calculate the cost of producing or delivering your products or services, also known as the cost of goods sold (COGS). This includes direct costs such as raw materials, labor, and production expenses. Calculate your COGS as a percentage of your projected revenue to determine the gross profit margin. This margin represents the profitability of your core operations.

3. Operating Expenses: Identify and estimate your operating expenses, which include both fixed and variable costs. Fixed costs include rent, utilities, salaries, insurance, and other expenses that do not vary with sales volume. Variable costs, on the other hand, fluctuate with sales or production levels, such as marketing expenses or cost of materials. Project your operating expenses on a monthly or annual basis and include them in your financial projections.

4. Cash Flow Projections: Create a cash flow projection to track the inflow and outflow of cash in your business. It allows you to forecast your cash position over time, taking into account revenue, expenses, and other factors that impact cash flow. This projection helps you understand when and how much cash you will need to cover expenses and identify potential cash flow gaps.

5. Profit and Loss Statement: Develop a profit and loss statement, also known as an income statement. It summarizes your revenue, COGS, gross profit, operating expenses, and net profit (or loss) over a specific period. The profit and loss statement provides an overview of your business's financial performance and its ability to generate profits.

6. Balance Sheet: Create a balance sheet that presents your business's financial position at a specific point in time. It includes your assets (such as cash, inventory, equipment, and accounts receivable), liabilities (such as loans, accounts payable, and accrued expenses), and owner's equity. The balance sheet provides a snapshot of your business's financial health and its net worth.

7. Break-Even Analysis: Perform a break-even analysis to determine the point at which your business's revenue equals its total costs, resulting in neither profit nor loss. This analysis helps you understand the minimum level of sales needed to cover your costs and start generating profits. It can also provide insights into the viability of your business model and pricing strategy.

8. Budgeting: Based on your financial projections, develop a budget that outlines your planned income and expenses over a specific period. The budget serves as a financial roadmap, guiding your spending and ensuring that you allocate resources effectively. It helps you set financial targets, control costs, and make informed decisions regarding investments, hiring, marketing, and other business activities.

9. **Sensitivity Analysis:** Conduct sensitivity analysis to assess how changes in key variables, such as sales volume or pricing, can impact your financial projections. This analysis allows you to understand the potential risks and uncertainties associated with your financial projections and make contingency plans to mitigate them.

10. **Review and Update:** Regularly review and update your financial projections and budget as your business evolves. Compare your actual financial performance against your projections and make adjustments

Chapter 4
Building a Strong Foundation

Introduction

Building a strong foundation is crucial for the long-term success of any entrepreneurial venture. It involves establishing a solid framework that supports the growth and sustainability of your business. In this section, we will explore the key elements involved in building a strong foundation for your venture, from setting up proper legal and operational structures to developing effective leadership and organizational practices.

1. Legal and Regulatory Compliance: Ensure that your business complies with all relevant laws and regulations. This includes registering your business entity, obtaining necessary licenses and permits, and adhering to tax and employment regulations. By meeting legal requirements, you establish credibility, mitigate risks, and build a solid foundation for growth.

2. Organizational Structure: Define your organizational structure to establish clear lines of authority, roles, and responsibilities. Determine the key positions and functions required for your business operations and consider factors such as scalability, efficiency, and delegation of tasks. A well-defined organizational structure fosters effective communication, coordination, and accountability within your team.

3. Leadership and Team Building: As an entrepreneur, your leadership plays a critical role in building a strong foundation. Develop your leadership skills, set a clear vision for your business,

and cultivate a positive and inclusive work culture. Build a talented team that shares your vision and values, and invest in their growth and development. Effective leadership and a cohesive team contribute to the success and sustainability of your venture.

4. Operational Processes and Systems: Establish efficient operational processes and systems to streamline your business operations. Document standard operating procedures (SOPs) for key tasks, implement quality control measures, and leverage technology to automate and optimize processes wherever possible. Well-defined operational processes enhance productivity, consistency, and customer satisfaction.

5. Risk Management: Identify and mitigate potential risks that could impact your business. Conduct a thorough risk assessment to identify operational, financial, legal, and market risks. Develop strategies to minimize these risks and create contingency plans to address unforeseen challenges. By proactively managing risks, you safeguard your business and maintain its resilience.

6. Financial Management: Implement sound financial management practices to ensure the financial health and stability of your business. Develop and adhere to a realistic budget, regularly monitor cash flow, and maintain accurate financial records. Seek professional advice when needed, such as from accountants or financial advisors, to make informed financial decisions and optimize your resources.

7. Customer Relationship Management: Focus on building strong relationships with your customers. Develop a customer-centric approach by understanding their needs, providing exceptional service, and actively seeking feedback. Implement customer relationship management (CRM) systems to track customer interactions, personalize communication, and nurture long-term customer loyalty.

8. **Branding and Marketing:** Build a strong brand presence and develop effective marketing strategies to reach and engage your target audience. Define your brand identity, positioning, and messaging. Utilize various marketing channels, both online and offline, to create awareness, generate leads, and drive sales. Consistent and compelling branding and marketing efforts contribute to the visibility and success of your business.

9. **Continuous Learning and Adaptation:** Embrace a mindset of continuous learning and adaptation. Stay updated on industry trends, market dynamics, and emerging technologies. Seek feedback from customers, employees, and industry experts to identify areas for improvement and innovation. Be willing to pivot and adapt your strategies as needed to stay ahead in a dynamic business landscape.

Building a strong foundation sets the stage for your entrepreneurial venture's success and growth. By establishing proper legal and operational structures, developing effective leadership and organizational practices, and focusing on key areas such as risk management, financial management, customer relationships, and branding, you create a solid framework for long-term sustainability and achievement of your business goals.

4.1 Selecting the Right Legal Structure

Selecting the right legal structure is a crucial decision when building a strong foundation for your entrepreneurial venture. The legal structure you choose will impact your business's taxes, liability, ownership, and operational flexibility. In this section, we will explore the different legal structures commonly used by entrepreneurs and the factors to consider when selecting the most suitable option for your business.

1. Sole Proprietorship: A sole proprietorship is the simplest and most common form of legal structure. It involves a single individual who owns and operates the business. As a sole proprietor, you have complete control over the business, but you are personally liable for its debts and legal obligations. This structure is relatively easy and inexpensive to set up, but it offers no separation between personal and business assets.

2. Partnership: A partnership is a legal structure that involves two or more individuals who share ownership and responsibilities for the business. There are two main types of partnerships: general partnerships and limited partnerships. In a general partnership, all partners have equal rights and liabilities. In a limited partnership, there are general partners who manage the business and have unlimited liability, and limited partners who contribute capital but have limited liability. Partnerships offer shared decision-making and shared profits, but partners are personally liable for the partnership's debts.

3. Limited Liability Company (LLC): An LLC is a popular legal structure that combines the benefits of a partnership and a corporation. It provides limited liability protection to its owners, known as members, while offering flexibility in terms of management and taxation. Members are not personally liable for the company's

debts, and the company's income is typically taxed at the individual level. Forming an LLC requires filing articles of organization with the appropriate state agency and creating an operating agreement that outlines the company's internal rules and management structure.

4. Corporation: A corporation is a separate legal entity that offers the highest level of liability protection for its owners, known as shareholders. Shareholders are not personally liable for the corporation's debts or legal obligations. Corporations have a more complex structure and require strict compliance with legal formalities, such as holding regular shareholder meetings and maintaining accurate financial records. There are two main types of corporations: C corporations and S corporations. C corporations are subject to double taxation, where both the corporation and shareholders are taxed on profits. S corporations, on the other hand, pass profits and losses through to shareholders' personal tax returns, avoiding double taxation.

5. Nonprofit Organization: If your entrepreneurial venture has a charitable, educational, or social purpose, you may consider forming a nonprofit organization. Nonprofits are structured to serve public or community interests and are eligible for tax-exempt status. The process of forming a nonprofit involves registering with the appropriate state agency, obtaining tax-exempt status from the Internal Revenue Service (IRS), and adhering to specific regulations and reporting requirements.

When selecting the right legal structure for your business, consider the following factors:

- Liability Protection: Evaluate the level of personal liability you are willing to assume. Sole proprietorships and partnerships offer less protection, while LLCs and corporations provide limited liability to their owners.

- Taxes: Consider the tax implications of each legal structure. Different structures have varying tax treatment, so consult with a tax professional to understand the tax obligations associated with each option.

- Ownership and Control: Determine how you want to structure ownership and decision-making within your business. Some legal structures, such as corporations, allow for the issuance of different classes of stock and have more formal governance structures.

- Operational Flexibility: Consider the level of flexibility you need in managing and operating your business. Some structures, like sole proprietorships and partnerships, offer more flexibility, while corporations have stricter governance requirements.

- Future Plans: Think about your long-term goals for your business. If you plan to

4.2 Registering Your Business

Registering your business is a crucial step in establishing a strong foundation for your entrepreneurial venture. It involves formally establishing your business's legal existence and complying with the necessary government regulations. Registering your business provides various benefits, including legal protection, credibility, and access to certain privileges and resources. In this section, we will explore the process of registering your business and the key considerations involved.

1. Choose a Business Name: Select a unique and memorable name for your business. Ensure that the name aligns with your brand identity and is not already in use by another business. Conduct a

thorough search to check the availability of the name and any potential conflicts or trademark infringement issues.

2. Determine the Business Structure: Decide on the legal structure that best suits your business. Consider factors such as liability protection, taxation, ownership, and operational flexibility. Common options include sole proprietorship, partnership, limited liability company (LLC), and corporation. Each structure has its own requirements and implications, so consult with a legal professional or business advisor to make an informed decision.

3. Obtain an Employer Identification Number (EIN): An Employer Identification Number (EIN) is a unique nine-digit identifier issued by the Internal Revenue Service (IRS) for tax purposes. Most businesses, except sole proprietorships with no employees, need an EIN. You can apply for an EIN online through the IRS website.

4. Register with the Secretary of State: Depending on your business structure, you may need to register with the Secretary of State or similar state agency. This step is typically required for partnerships, LLCs, and corporations. The registration process varies by state, but it generally involves filing the necessary forms and paying the required fees. Check with your state's Secretary of State office for specific requirements.

5. Apply for Business Licenses and Permits: Determine the licenses and permits required to operate your business legally. The specific licenses and permits depend on various factors such as your industry, location, and the nature of your business activities. Research the requirements at the federal, state, and local levels, and apply for the necessary licenses and permits accordingly.

6. Register for State and Local Taxes: Understand the tax obligations for your business at the state and local levels. This may include sales tax, income tax, property tax, and employment tax. Register with the

appropriate tax agencies and obtain the necessary tax identification numbers.

7. Trademarks, Copyrights, and Patents: Consider protecting your intellectual property rights through trademarks, copyrights, and patents. If you have unique brand names, logos, or inventions, consult with an intellectual property attorney to determine the appropriate steps for registration and protection.

8. Obtain Business Insurance: Assess the insurance needs for your business and obtain the necessary coverage. Common types of business insurance include general liability insurance, property insurance, professional liability insurance, and workers' compensation insurance. Insurance provides protection against potential risks and can help safeguard your business's assets and operations.

9. Compliance with Employment Laws: If you plan to hire employees, familiarize yourself with the relevant employment laws and regulations. This includes adhering to labor laws, providing proper employee benefits, maintaining payroll records, and complying with anti-discrimination and workplace safety regulations.

10. Ongoing Compliance: Understand that registration is not a one-time task. Businesses are typically required to fulfill ongoing compliance requirements, such as filing annual reports, renewing licenses and permits, and maintaining accurate records. Stay informed about your compliance obligations and ensure timely fulfillment.

It is advisable to consult with legal professionals, accountants, or business advisors during the registration process to ensure that you meet all the legal requirements and comply with applicable regulations. Proper registration and compliance establish a strong legal foundation for your business and position it for long-term success.

4.3 Understanding Intellectual Property Rights

Intellectual property (IP) refers to the legal rights that protect creations of the mind, such as inventions, designs, literary and artistic works, symbols, names, and images. Understanding intellectual property rights is crucial for entrepreneurs to protect their innovations, build a competitive advantage, and prevent unauthorized use or exploitation of their intellectual assets. In this section, we will explore the different types of intellectual property and the steps involved in safeguarding these rights.

1. Trademarks: Trademarks are used to protect brand names, logos, and slogans that distinguish goods or services from competitors. Registering a trademark provides exclusive rights to use the mark and prevents others from using similar marks that may cause confusion among consumers. Conduct a thorough search to ensure the availability of your desired trademark, and file a trademark application with the appropriate intellectual property office in your jurisdiction.

2. Copyrights: Copyrights protect original creative works, such as literary, artistic, and musical works, as well as software, films, and architectural designs. Copyright automatically applies upon creation, but registering your copyright provides additional legal protection and evidence of ownership. Register your copyrights with the relevant copyright office to establish your rights and the date of creation.

3. Patents: Patents protect inventions and grant exclusive rights to the inventor for a limited period. There are three types of patents: utility patents (protecting new and useful processes, machines,

compositions of matter, and improvements), design patents (protecting new, original, and ornamental designs), and plant patents (protecting new varieties of plants). Obtaining a patent involves a detailed application process and examination by a patent office to assess the invention's novelty and non-obviousness.

4. Trade Secrets: Trade secrets refer to confidential and valuable information that gives a business a competitive advantage. Trade secrets can include formulas, processes, customer lists, marketing strategies, and other proprietary information. Unlike patents, trade secrets are not publicly disclosed and do not have a fixed duration of protection. To protect trade secrets, businesses must implement appropriate measures, such as confidentiality agreements and restricted access to sensitive information.

5. Licensing and Assignment: Entrepreneurs can monetize their intellectual property by licensing or assigning their rights to others. Licensing allows another party to use your IP under specific conditions, while retaining ownership. Assigning IP involves transferring the ownership rights to another party. These arrangements can be beneficial for generating revenue, expanding market reach, and leveraging expertise or resources of other entities.

6. International Considerations: If you plan to conduct business internationally, be aware that intellectual property rights vary across jurisdictions. Consider filing for protection in the countries where you operate or seek legal advice to navigate international IP laws and treaties, such as the Paris Convention for the Protection of Industrial Property and the World Intellectual Property Organization (WIPO) treaties.

7. Enforcement and Protection: Infringement of intellectual property rights can occur through unauthorized use, copying, or distribution. If you believe your IP rights have been violated, consult with legal professionals experienced in intellectual property law. They can help

you enforce your rights through cease and desist letters, negotiation, mediation, or litigation if necessary.

8. Continuous Monitoring and Management: Intellectual property requires ongoing management to ensure its protection and value. Regularly monitor for potential infringements, review the competitive landscape, and update your IP strategy accordingly. Consider working with IP professionals or attorneys to assist with portfolio management and renewal requirements.

Remember, intellectual property rights are valuable assets for your business, and protecting them is essential for maintaining a competitive edge. By understanding the different types of intellectual property, taking proactive steps to secure your rights, and enforcing them when necessary, you can safeguard your innovations, brand, and overall business interests.

4.4 Setting Up a Professional Network

Building a strong professional network is essential for entrepreneurs to establish valuable connections, gain industry insights, access resources, and create opportunities for collaboration and growth. A robust network can provide support, guidance, and potential partnerships that contribute to the success of your entrepreneurial venture. In this section, we will explore the importance of setting up a professional network and provide practical steps to help you build and nurture it effectively.

1. Define Your Goals: Clarify your objectives for building a professional network. Determine the specific industry, target audience, or expertise you want to connect with. Identifying your goals will help you focus your networking efforts and make strategic connections.

2. Attend Industry Events: Participate in conferences, trade shows, seminars, and workshops related to your industry. These events provide excellent opportunities to meet industry professionals, potential partners, and investors. Be proactive in networking by engaging in conversations, exchanging business cards, and following up with the people you meet.

3. Join Professional Associations: Become a member of relevant professional associations and organizations in your field. These associations often host events, conferences, and networking sessions exclusively for their members. Participate actively, volunteer for committees or leadership positions, and take advantage of the resources and networking opportunities they offer.

4. Utilize Online Platforms: Leverage social media and professional networking platforms such as LinkedIn to connect with industry professionals, entrepreneurs, and thought leaders. Create a compelling profile, join relevant groups, and engage in discussions. Share valuable content, provide insights, and reach out to individuals for virtual networking opportunities.

5. Attend Meetups and Networking Events: Explore local meetups and networking events tailored to entrepreneurs and professionals in your area. These gatherings provide a more intimate setting for networking and allow you to meet like-minded individuals who may share similar interests or challenges.

6. Seek Mentors and Advisors: Identify experienced professionals or entrepreneurs who can provide guidance and mentorship. Approach individuals whose expertise aligns with your business goals and seek their advice and insights. Building relationships with mentors and advisors can offer valuable guidance and support throughout your entrepreneurial journey.

7. **Engage in Online Communities:** Join online forums, discussion boards, and communities dedicated to entrepreneurship or specific industries. Participate actively, ask questions, share knowledge, and connect with fellow entrepreneurs. Online communities offer a platform to learn from others, seek advice, and expand your network beyond geographic boundaries.

8. **Collaborate and Partner:** Look for opportunities to collaborate with complementary businesses or entrepreneurs. Seek partnerships that align with your objectives and values. Collaborative projects can open doors to new networks, expand your reach, and provide access to shared resources.

9. **Follow Up and Maintain Relationships:** Networking is not just about making initial connections; it's about building and nurturing relationships over time. Follow up with individuals you meet, send personalized messages, and stay in touch. Offer support, share relevant information or resources, and look for ways to add value to your network.

10. **Give Back and Support Others:** Networking is a two-way street. Offer assistance, share your expertise, and support others in your network. Actively seek opportunities to connect people within your network who may benefit from collaborating or doing business together. By being a valuable resource and supporter, you strengthen your relationships and build a reputation as a trusted professional.

Remember, building a professional network takes time and effort. Be genuine, show interest in others, and focus on building meaningful connections. By expanding your network, you increase your chances of discovering new opportunities, gaining valuable insights, and accessing resources that can contribute to the success of your entrepreneurial endeavors.

Part II:
Launching Your Business

Chapter 5
Funding Your Venture

Introduction

Securing adequate funding is a critical aspect of turning your entrepreneurial dream into a reality. Whether you're starting a new business or expanding an existing one, having access to capital is essential for covering startup costs, operational expenses, research and development, marketing, and other necessary investments. In this section, we will explore various funding options available to entrepreneurs and provide insights on how to navigate the funding landscape effectively.

1. Self-Funding: One common way entrepreneurs fund their ventures is through self-funding, using personal savings, assets, or credit. Self-funding demonstrates your commitment to the business and allows you to maintain control over decision-making. However, it's important to carefully evaluate your financial situation and consider potential risks before investing your own resources.

2. Friends and Family: Another source of early-stage funding can be friends and family who believe in your vision. Approach your close network of trusted individuals who may be willing to invest in your business. When seeking funding from friends and family, it's crucial to maintain transparency, set clear expectations, and formalize agreements to protect relationships and avoid potential conflicts.

3. Angel Investors: Angel investors are high-net-worth individuals or groups who provide capital to startups in exchange for equity or convertible debt. These investors often have industry experience and

can offer valuable guidance and connections in addition to funding. To attract angel investors, prepare a compelling business plan, pitch deck, and financial projections that demonstrate the growth potential and viability of your venture.

4. Venture Capital: Venture capital firms invest in startups with high growth potential. They provide substantial funding in exchange for equity and typically play an active role in shaping the company's direction. Venture capital funding is often sought by businesses in technology, biotech, and other innovative sectors. To attract venture capital, demonstrate a scalable business model, a strong management team, and a clear path to profitability.

5. Crowdfunding: Crowdfunding platforms allow entrepreneurs to raise funds from a large number of individuals who contribute small amounts. This approach can be an effective way to validate your product or service, build a community of supporters, and access capital. There are different types of crowdfunding, including rewards-based (where backers receive non-equity rewards), equity-based (where backers become shareholders), and donation-based (where backers contribute without expecting financial returns).

6. Grants and Government Programs: Explore grants and government programs that offer funding for specific industries, research projects, or social initiatives. These programs may provide non-repayable funds or low-interest loans. Research local, regional, and national grant opportunities that align with your business goals and apply for funding that matches your venture's objectives.

7. Bank Loans and Credit: Traditional bank loans and lines of credit can be options for funding your business. Approach banks or financial institutions to explore the terms and requirements for small business loans. Prepare a detailed business plan, financial statements, and collateral to support your loan application. Consider

alternative lenders or online platforms that offer more flexible loan options for startups.

8. Business Incubators and Accelerators: Joining a business incubator or accelerator program can provide not only funding but also valuable resources, mentorship, and networking opportunities. These programs are designed to support early-stage businesses and help them grow rapidly. Research and apply to reputable incubators or accelerators that align with your industry and business objectives.

9. Strategic Partnerships: Explore strategic partnerships with established companies in your industry or complementary sectors. Strategic partnerships can provide access to funding, distribution channels, expertise, and a wider customer base. Identify potential partners who share a common vision or can offer synergistic benefits to your business.

10. Bootstrapping and Lean Startup Principles: Consider adopting a lean startup approach, focusing on minimal viable products and incremental growth. Bootstrapping involves operating with limited resources and finding creative ways to minimize

expenses. By demonstrating traction and generating revenue through lean practices, you may attract funding from investors or lenders at a later stage.

Remember, funding is a critical component of your entrepreneurial journey, and choosing the right funding option requires careful consideration. Evaluate your business needs, research the available funding sources, and tailor your approach based on your venture's stage, industry, and growth plans. Be prepared to pitch your business idea, demonstrate market potential, and showcase your ability to execute your plans effectively. By exploring multiple funding avenues and leveraging the support of investors or lenders, you can secure the financial resources necessary to bring your entrepreneurial vision to life.

5.1 Bootstrapping vs. External Financing

When it comes to funding your venture, entrepreneurs have two primary options: bootstrapping or seeking external financing. Each approach has its advantages and considerations, and the choice depends on various factors such as your business model, growth plans, risk tolerance, and available resources. In this section, we will explore the concepts of bootstrapping and external financing, highlighting their pros and cons to help you make an informed decision.

1. Bootstrapping:

Bootstrapping refers to funding your venture with your own personal savings, revenue generated by the business, or through cost-cutting measures. This approach allows you to maintain complete control over your business without diluting equity or incurring debt. Here are some key aspects of bootstrapping:

- Self-reliance: Bootstrapping requires you to be self-reliant and resourceful. You rely on your own financial means and creative problem-solving to fund and grow your business.

- Control: By self-funding, you retain full control over decision-making, strategic direction, and the pace of growth. You're not beholden to external investors or lenders.

- Financial Discipline: Bootstrapping encourages financial discipline as you carefully manage expenses, prioritize spending, and focus on generating revenue early on.

- Slow Growth: Funding limitations in bootstrapping may result in slower growth compared to ventures with external financing. You may need to prioritize certain activities and scale gradually.

- Risk and Personal Liability: Bootstrapping involves personal financial risk. If the business fails, you may bear the consequences personally, and your personal assets could be at stake.

2. External Financing:

External financing involves seeking funding from external sources such as investors, venture capitalists, banks, or government programs. Here are some considerations when opting for external financing:

- Capital Injection: External financing provides a significant capital injection, allowing for faster growth, scalability, and the ability to seize market opportunities.

- Expertise and Networks: External investors often bring valuable expertise, industry connections, and mentorship to help your business succeed. They can offer guidance and open doors to potential customers, partners, or strategic alliances.

- Dilution of Ownership: When seeking external financing, you typically need to offer equity or a share of profits, which dilutes your ownership and control over the business. It's important to carefully consider the trade-off between funding and ownership.

- Debt Obligations: If you choose to finance your venture through loans or credit, you'll have to meet repayment obligations, which can impact your cash flow and financial flexibility.

- Investor Expectations: External investors often have expectations for a return on their investment. They may influence strategic decisions, require regular reporting, and have a say in the direction of the business.

- Validation and Credibility: Securing external financing can provide validation and enhance your credibility in the eyes of stakeholders, customers, and partners. It demonstrates market interest and confidence in your business concept.

It's worth noting that bootstrapping and external financing are not mutually exclusive. Many entrepreneurs start by bootstrapping their ventures and later seek external funding to accelerate growth. Ultimately, the choice between bootstrapping and external financing depends on your specific circumstances and goals.

Consider the nature of your business, your financial situation, the competitive landscape, and the growth trajectory you envision. Evaluate the advantages and trade-offs of each approach and determine the most suitable funding strategy for your entrepreneurial journey. Remember that flexibility and adaptability are key, and it's essential to regularly reassess your funding options as your business evolves.

5.2 Exploring Funding Options

When it comes to funding your entrepreneurial venture, there are various options available beyond bootstrapping or external financing. Exploring different funding sources can increase your chances of securing the capital you need to bring your business idea to life. In this section, we will explore additional funding options that entrepreneurs can consider:

1. Grants and Awards: Research and apply for grants and business awards that are specific to your industry, location, or the nature of your venture. These can be offered by government agencies, non-profit organizations, or private foundations. Grants and awards often provide non-repayable funds that can be used to cover startup costs, research and development, or other business expenses.

2. Crowdfunding: Crowdfunding platforms have gained popularity as an alternative way to raise capital. By presenting your business idea or product to a broad audience, you can attract individuals who are willing to contribute small amounts of money. There are different types of crowdfunding, including rewards-based (offering non-financial rewards to backers), equity-based (offering equity shares to backers), and donation-based (collecting donations without offering rewards or equity).

3. Incubators and Accelerators: Joining a business incubator or accelerator program can provide not only funding but also valuable resources, mentorship, and access to a network of entrepreneurs and investors. These programs are designed to support early-stage ventures and help them grow rapidly. Incubators and accelerators often offer seed funding, co-working spaces, mentorship, and various business support services.

4. Corporate Sponsorships and Partnerships: Explore opportunities for corporate sponsorships or partnerships with established companies in your industry. Corporations may be interested in supporting innovative startups and may provide funding, resources, or access to their customer base. Look for corporate-sponsored incubators, accelerators, or programs that offer financial support and mentorship.

5. Business Competitions: Participating in business competitions can not only provide funding opportunities but also offer exposure, networking, and valuable feedback on your business idea. Many universities, organizations, and companies host business competitions where entrepreneurs pitch their ventures to win monetary prizes or investment opportunities.

6. Small Business Loans and Microfinance: Investigate small business loans offered by banks, credit unions, or online lending platforms. These loans are specifically designed to meet the funding needs of small businesses and startups. Additionally, microfinance institutions provide small loans to entrepreneurs who may not qualify for traditional bank loans, especially in underserved communities or developing regions.

7. Business Grants from Corporations: Some corporations offer grants or funding programs to support startups and small businesses in specific industries or sectors. These grants can provide capital, mentorship, and access to corporate resources. Research corporate grant programs that align with your business and apply for funding.

8. Angel Networks: Angel networks are groups of individual angel investors who collectively invest in early-stage ventures. These networks can provide a valuable source of capital and expertise. Research and reach out to angel networks in your industry or location and pitch your business idea to secure funding.

9. Peer-to-Peer Lending: Peer-to-peer lending platforms connect borrowers with individual lenders who are willing to provide loans. These platforms facilitate lending transactions, often at competitive interest rates. Peer-to-peer lending can be an alternative to traditional bank loans, particularly for startups or entrepreneurs who may face challenges in securing financing from traditional sources.

10. Government Programs and Economic Development Initiatives: Governments often have programs and initiatives aimed at promoting entrepreneurship and supporting small businesses. These programs can include grants, low-interest loans, tax incentives, or business development services. Research the resources available at the local, regional, and national levels to identify relevant government programs that can provide funding support.

Remember, when exploring funding options, it's essential to conduct thorough research, understand the terms and conditions, and evaluate the fit with your business goals. Prepare a compelling business plan, financial projections, and a persuasive pitch to increase your chances of securing funding. Be proactive in networking, attending industry events, and building relationships with potential investors or funding sources. By exploring a variety of funding options, you can increase your chances of finding the capital you need to turn your entrepreneurial dream into a reality.

5.3 Crafting an Effective Pitch Deck

A pitch deck is a powerful tool for entrepreneurs seeking funding for their ventures. It is a visual presentation that showcases your business idea, value proposition, market opportunity, and financial projections to potential investors. A well-crafted pitch deck can captivate investors and spark their interest in your venture. In this section, we will explore the key elements of an effective pitch deck:

1. Problem Statement: Start by clearly articulating the problem or pain point that your product or service aims to solve. Explain the significance of the problem, its impact on customers, and any existing solutions' limitations. This sets the stage for showcasing the unique value of your venture.

2. Solution: Present your solution and explain how it addresses the identified problem. Highlight the key features and benefits of your product or service. Use visuals, prototypes, or demos to demonstrate the functionality and effectiveness of your solution. Clearly communicate how your offering is different and better than existing alternatives.

3. Market Opportunity: Provide a compelling overview of the market opportunity for your venture. Present market size, growth trends, and target customer segments. Include data, market research, and customer insights to support your claims. Convey a clear understanding of the target market's needs, preferences, and behaviors.

4. Business Model: Explain your business model and how you plan to generate revenue. Describe your pricing strategy, distribution channels, and customer acquisition approach. Highlight any competitive advantages, such as proprietary technology, intellectual property, or strategic partnerships.

5. Marketing and Sales Strategy: Outline your marketing and sales strategy to attract and retain customers. Describe your customer acquisition channels, marketing campaigns, and sales tactics. Highlight any early traction or validation, such as customer testimonials, pilot programs, or initial sales figures.

6. Competition and Differentiation: Conduct a thorough analysis of your competitors and clearly articulate your unique value proposition. Showcase your competitive advantages, such as superior technology, cost efficiencies, or a differentiated customer experience. Highlight any barriers to entry or intellectual property protection that give your venture a competitive edge.

7. Team and Advisors: Introduce your team and highlight their relevant expertise and experience. Showcase key team members' backgrounds, qualifications, and achievements. Mention any advisors, mentors, or industry experts who support your venture. Investors often consider the strength and capabilities of the founding team when making funding decisions.

8. Financial Projections: Present your financial projections, including revenue forecasts, profitability targets, and key financial metrics. Outline the assumptions behind your projections and the milestones you aim to achieve. Be realistic, transparent, and show a clear path to profitability. If applicable, include information on previous funding rounds or existing investors.

9. Funding Request and Use of Funds: Clearly state the amount of funding you are seeking and how the funds will be used to accelerate the growth of your venture. Be specific about the allocation of funds for product development, marketing, hiring, or other strategic initiatives. Demonstrate a solid understanding of your capital requirements and the expected return on investment for potential investors.

10. Conclusion and Call to Action: Summarize the key points of your pitch and end with a strong call to action. Encourage investors to engage further by scheduling meetings, providing additional information, or expressing their interest in participating in your funding round.

Remember, a pitch deck should be concise, visually appealing, and engaging. Use clear and compelling language, visuals, and storytelling techniques to capture investors' attention and create an emotional connection with your venture. Practice your pitch to ensure a confident and convincing delivery. Tailor your pitch deck for each investor or audience, emphasizing aspects that align with their investment criteria or interests. A well-crafted pitch deck can significantly enhance your chances of securing funding and attracting the right investors to support your entrepreneurial journey.

5.4 Securing Investments or Loans

Securing investments or loans for your entrepreneurial venture is a critical step in turning your business idea into a reality. It requires careful planning, preparation, and effective communication with potential investors or lenders. In this section, we will explore key steps and considerations to help you secure investments or loans:

1. Refine Your Business Plan: Ensure that your business plan is well-developed, comprehensive, and aligned with your funding goals. Update your financial projections, market analysis, and competitive strategy based on the latest information and insights. Fine-tune your value proposition and articulate the growth potential of your venture.

2. Identify Potential Investors or Lenders: Research and identify potential investors or lenders who are interested in your industry, stage of business, and funding needs. Seek out individuals or organizations that have a track record of investing in similar ventures or supporting entrepreneurs in your sector.

3. Network and Build Relationships: Attend industry events, networking functions, and pitch competitions to connect with potential investors or lenders. Build relationships, seek introductions, and engage in conversations to generate interest in your venture. Leverage your existing network, mentors, or advisors for referrals and introductions to potential funding sources.

4. Prepare an Investment or Loan Package: Develop a comprehensive investment or loan package that includes your business plan, financial projections, market analysis, and other relevant documents. Customize the package for each potential investor or lender, highlighting aspects that align with their specific interests or investment criteria. Clearly outline the terms, conditions, and potential return on investment.

5. Deliver a Compelling Pitch: Craft a compelling pitch presentation that communicates the value proposition of your venture, market opportunity, competitive advantage, and financial projections. Tailor your pitch to the specific needs and interests of each potential investor or lender. Practice your pitch to ensure a confident and persuasive delivery.

6. Due Diligence: Be prepared for potential investors or lenders to conduct due diligence on your venture. They may request additional information, financial statements, legal documentation, or customer references. Respond promptly and provide the requested information in a professional and transparent manner.

7. **Negotiate Terms:** If there is interest from investors or lenders, be prepared to negotiate the terms of the investment or loan. Understand the implications of different funding structures, such as equity financing, convertible notes, or debt financing. Seek legal or financial advice to ensure you make informed decisions and protect your interests.

8. **Legal and Financial Documentation:** Once you have reached an agreement with investors or lenders, work with legal and financial professionals to draft and finalize the necessary legal and financial documentation. Ensure that all parties involved have a clear understanding of the terms, rights, and obligations associated with the investment or loan.

9. **Follow-Up and Relationship Management:** Maintain regular communication and updates with your investors or lenders. Provide progress reports, financial statements, and other relevant information to keep them informed about the performance of your venture. Building strong relationships and demonstrating transparency can increase your chances of securing additional funding in the future.

10. **Execute Your Plan:** Once you secure investments or loans, execute your business plan with a focus on achieving key milestones and targets. Monitor your progress, adjust your strategy as needed, and provide regular updates to your investors or lenders. Building a track record of success and meeting or exceeding expectations can increase your credibility and potentially attract additional funding opportunities.

Remember, securing investments or loans is a process that requires persistence, resilience, and effective communication. Be prepared for rejections and setbacks along the way, but remain focused on finding the right investors or lenders who believe in your vision and are aligned with your goals. Continuously refine your pitch, leverage your network, and adapt your approach based on feedback and market dynamics. **With a well-prepared plan, a compelling pitch, and a strategic mindset, you can increase your chances of securing the investments or loans necessary to fuel the growth of your entrepreneurial venture.**

Chapter 6
Building a Winning Team

Introduction

Building a winning team is a crucial aspect of entrepreneurial success. No matter how innovative your business idea or how promising your market opportunity, the success of your venture ultimately depends on the people behind it. In this section, we will explore the key considerations and strategies for building a winning team that can drive your business forward.

A winning team is composed of individuals who not only possess the necessary skills and expertise but also share a common vision, values, and passion for the venture. They work together cohesively, complementing each other's strengths and filling in any skill gaps. Here are some essential steps to help you build a winning team:

1. Define Roles and Responsibilities: Clearly define the roles and responsibilities needed to execute your business plan. Identify the key functions, such as operations, marketing, sales, finance, and product development. Determine the specific skill sets, qualifications, and experience required for each role.

2. Recruit Top Talent: Attracting top talent is essential for building a winning team. Utilize multiple channels to recruit potential team members, including online job platforms, industry networks, referrals, and partnerships with educational institutions. Develop a compelling employer brand that showcases your company culture, mission, and growth potential.

3. Conduct Effective Interviews: Conduct thorough interviews to assess candidates' skills, experience, and cultural fit. Use a combination of behavioral and situational questions to evaluate their problem-solving abilities, teamwork skills, and alignment with your company's values. Consider conducting multiple rounds of interviews to ensure a comprehensive evaluation.

4. Assess Cultural Fit: Cultural fit is critical for team cohesion and long-term success. Assess candidates' alignment with your company's values, vision, and work culture. Look for individuals who demonstrate adaptability, resilience, and a growth mindset. Consider involving multiple team members in the interview process to gauge cultural fit from different perspectives.

5. Encourage Diversity and Inclusion: Strive for diversity and inclusion within your team. Embrace different perspectives, backgrounds, and experiences. Diversity fosters innovation, creativity, and a broader understanding of your target market. Create an inclusive and welcoming environment where everyone feels valued and has equal opportunities for growth and advancement.

6. Foster a Collaborative Environment: Cultivate a collaborative work environment where team members can openly communicate, share ideas, and contribute to decision-making. Encourage cross-functional collaboration and teamwork, as it promotes synergy and maximizes the collective expertise of your team. Foster a culture of continuous learning and professional development.

7. Provide Clear Goals and Expectations: Set clear goals, objectives, and performance expectations for each team member. Establish key performance indicators (KPIs) and metrics to track progress and measure success. Regularly communicate expectations and provide constructive feedback to ensure alignment and accountability.

8. Support Professional Development: Invest in the professional development of your team members. Provide opportunities for training, workshops, conferences, and mentorship programs. Encourage them to expand their knowledge, develop new skills, and stay updated with industry trends. Supporting their growth demonstrates your commitment to their success and fosters loyalty and engagement.

9. Promote a Positive Work Culture: Cultivate a positive work culture that values work-life balance, employee well-being, and recognition for achievements. Celebrate successes, encourage open communication, and promote a supportive and inclusive atmosphere. Regular team-building activities, social events, and employee appreciation initiatives can contribute to a positive work culture.

10. Retain and Reward Top Performers: Retaining top performers is vital for the long-term success of your venture. Recognize and reward exceptional performance through competitive compensation packages, performance-based bonuses, stock options, or other incentives. Provide opportunities for growth, advancement, and increased responsibility within the company.

Building a winning team is an ongoing process. Continuously assess the team dynamics, address

any conflicts or challenges, and adapt your strategies as your business evolves. Remember, a winning team is not just a group of individuals but a cohesive unit that shares a common vision, works towards shared goals, and thrives in a supportive and collaborative environment.

6.1 Hiring the Right People

Hiring the right people is a critical step in building a winning team for your entrepreneurial venture. Each team member plays a significant role in shaping the success and growth of your business. In this section, we will explore key strategies and considerations for hiring the right people:

1. Clearly Define the Job Requirements: Before initiating the hiring process, clearly define the job requirements and the specific skills, qualifications, and experience needed for the role. Determine the core competencies, technical skills, and soft skills that are essential for success in the position.

2. Develop a Compelling Job Description: Craft a compelling job description that accurately represents the role, responsibilities, and expectations. Clearly communicate the qualifications, key tasks, and the value proposition of working for your venture. Highlight the unique aspects of your company culture and the opportunities for growth and impact.

3. Utilize Multiple Sourcing Channels: Cast a wide net to attract a diverse pool of candidates by utilizing multiple sourcing channels. These can include online job platforms, industry-specific networks, social media, referrals from employees or industry contacts, and partnerships with educational institutions or professional organizations.

4. Screen Resumes and Applications: Screen resumes and applications to identify candidates who meet the basic qualifications for the position. Look for relevant experience, educational background, and achievements that align with the job requirements. Pay attention to attention to detail, clarity of communication, and the candidate's ability to articulate their skills and experience.

5. **Conduct Effective Interviews:** Conduct interviews to assess candidates' fit for the role and alignment with your company culture. Prepare a structured interview process with a combination of behavioral, situational, and competency-based questions. Evaluate candidates' problem-solving abilities, teamwork skills, and their potential for growth within the organization.

6. **Assess Cultural Fit:** Cultural fit is crucial for team cohesion and long-term success. Assess candidates' alignment with your company's values, vision, and work culture during the interview process. Look for individuals who demonstrate adaptability, a growth mindset, and a willingness to contribute positively to the team dynamics.

7. **Perform Skills Assessments and Tests:** Depending on the nature of the role, consider conducting skills assessments or tests to evaluate candidates' abilities and competencies. This can include technical assessments, case studies, or sample work assignments. These assessments provide valuable insights into candidates' practical skills and problem-solving capabilities.

8. **Involve Multiple Stakeholders:** Involve multiple stakeholders in the hiring process to gain different perspectives and insights. This can include members of the team, senior leaders, or representatives from other departments. Each stakeholder can provide valuable input and help ensure a well-rounded evaluation of candidates.

9. **Check References:** Before making a final decision, conduct reference checks to validate the information provided by candidates and gain insights into their work ethic, performance, and interpersonal skills. Contact previous employers, colleagues, or mentors who can provide relevant feedback on the candidate's abilities and suitability for the role.

10. Trust Your Instincts: While it's important to consider qualifications and experience, trust your instincts when making hiring decisions. Assess the candidate's enthusiasm, passion, and alignment with your vision. Look for individuals who are eager to learn, adaptable, and willing to contribute to the growth of your venture.

Remember, hiring the right people is not just about finding individuals with the necessary skills and qualifications. It's also about finding candidates who align with your company's values, culture, and long-term goals. Take the time to carefully evaluate candidates, involve multiple perspectives, and trust your instincts to ensure that you hire individuals who can contribute to building a winning team for your entrepreneurial journey.

6.2 Creating a Company Culture

Creating a strong and positive company culture is essential for building a winning team and driving the success of your entrepreneurial venture. Company culture encompasses the shared values, beliefs, behaviors, and norms that shape the work environment and guide how individuals interact and work together. In this section, we will explore key strategies for creating a company culture that fosters teamwork, engagement, and growth:

1. Define Your Core Values: Start by defining your core values as the foundation of your company culture. These are the guiding principles that define the character, ethics, and priorities of your organization. Ensure that your core values are aligned with your mission and vision, and communicate them clearly to your team.

2. Lead by Example: As a leader, your actions and behaviors have a significant impact on shaping the company culture. Lead by example and embody the values you want to see in your team. Demonstrate

integrity, transparency, respect, and a strong work ethic. Cultivate a positive and inclusive environment where everyone feels valued and supported.

3. Foster Open Communication: Encourage open and transparent communication at all levels of the organization. Create channels and platforms for employees to share ideas, provide feedback, and raise concerns. Foster a culture where individuals feel comfortable expressing their opinions and collaborating on solutions.

4. Promote Collaboration and Teamwork: Foster a collaborative work environment where team members can work together towards common goals. Encourage cross-functional collaboration and teamwork, breaking down silos and promoting knowledge sharing. Recognize and celebrate team achievements, fostering a sense of unity and shared purpose.

5. Empower and Delegate: Empower your team members by delegating responsibilities and giving them the autonomy to make decisions and contribute their unique skills and expertise. Trust in their abilities and provide support and guidance when needed. Encourage a sense of ownership and accountability.

6. Invest in Employee Development: Support the growth and development of your team members. Provide opportunities for training, skill-building workshops, and professional development programs. Encourage employees to pursue their career goals and acquire new knowledge and skills. Recognize and reward their efforts and achievements.

7. Promote Work-Life Balance: Foster a healthy work-life balance by promoting flexibility and well-being. Encourage employees to take breaks, prioritize self-care, and maintain a healthy work-life integration. Consider implementing policies and programs that

support work-life balance, such as flexible working hours or remote work options.

8. Recognize and Appreciate: Regularly recognize and appreciate the contributions and achievements of your team members. Celebrate milestones, acknowledge hard work, and provide constructive feedback. Implement recognition programs or initiatives that highlight outstanding performance and reinforce a culture of appreciation.

9. Embrace Diversity and Inclusion: Embrace diversity and inclusion within your company culture. Create an environment where individuals from different backgrounds, experiences, and perspectives feel welcome and valued. Foster an inclusive culture that encourages diversity of thought, promotes innovation, and fosters a broader understanding of your target market.

10. Regularly Assess and Evolve: Continuously assess and evaluate your company culture to ensure that it remains aligned with your values, goals, and the needs of your team. Seek feedback from employees through surveys, focus groups, or one-on-one conversations. Use the insights gained to make improvements and evolve your company culture over time.

Remember that building a strong company culture is an ongoing effort that requires commitment, consistency, and adaptability. It sets the tone for your organization, influences how your team members work together, and attracts and retains top talent. By intentionally shaping and nurturing a positive company culture, you can create an environment that inspires and empowers your team to achieve greatness.

6.3 Effective Team Management

Effective team management is crucial for harnessing the full potential of your winning team and achieving optimal results in your entrepreneurial venture. As a leader, it is your responsibility to guide, support, and motivate your team members to work together cohesively and deliver their best performance. In this section, we will explore key strategies for effective team management:

1. Set Clear Goals and Expectations: Clearly define the goals and expectations for your team. Ensure that each team member understands their role in achieving these goals and the specific outcomes they are responsible for. Set SMART (Specific, Measurable, Achievable, Relevant, Time-bound) goals to provide clarity and focus.

2. Communicate Openly and Transparently: Foster open and transparent communication within your team. Share relevant information, updates, and decisions in a timely manner. Encourage two-way communication and active listening. Create an environment where team members feel comfortable expressing their ideas, concerns, and feedback.

3. Delegate Responsibility: Delegate tasks and responsibilities to team members based on their skills, expertise, and development goals. Trust your team members to deliver and empower them with the necessary authority and resources. Regularly review progress, provide guidance and support, and be available to address any questions or challenges.

4. Encourage Collaboration and Teamwork: Promote collaboration and teamwork within your team. Encourage knowledge sharing, cross-functional collaboration, and peer support. Foster a culture where individuals value and respect each other's contributions.

Facilitate team-building activities and create opportunities for team members to collaborate on projects or initiatives.

5. Provide Feedback and Recognition: Offer regular feedback to your team members on their performance, highlighting their strengths and areas for improvement. Provide constructive feedback that is specific, actionable, and focused on growth. Recognize and appreciate their efforts and achievements publicly and privately. Celebrate milestones and successes together.

6. Support Professional Development: Invest in the professional development of your team members. Identify their growth areas and provide opportunities for training, mentorship, and skill enhancement. Encourage them to take on new challenges and responsibilities that align with their career aspirations. Support their personal and professional growth.

7. Foster a Positive Work Environment: Create a positive work environment that promotes productivity, collaboration, and well-being. Encourage work-life balance and provide resources and support for the physical and mental well-being of your team members. Foster a culture of respect, inclusivity, and support, where diversity is celebrated.

8. Address Conflict and Challenges: Proactively address conflicts and challenges within your team. Encourage open dialogue and provide a safe space for team members to express their concerns. Mediate conflicts and facilitate resolution by encouraging active listening, empathy, and finding win-win solutions. Address issues promptly to prevent escalation.

9. Lead by Example: As a team leader, lead by example. Demonstrate the behaviors and work ethic you expect from your team members. Show integrity, accountability, and professionalism. Be approachable,

supportive, and accessible. Act as a role model and inspire your team through your actions and attitude.

10. **Continuously Learn and Improve:** Embrace a mindset of continuous learning and improvement. Seek feedback from your team members on your leadership style and areas for growth. Reflect on your own performance and identify opportunities for development. Stay updated with industry trends and best practices in team management.

Effective team management requires a combination of leadership skills, effective communication, and a genuine commitment to the growth and well-being of your team members. By implementing these strategies, you can create a positive work environment, foster collaboration, and inspire your team to achieve exceptional results in your entrepreneurial journey.

6.4 Motivating and Retaining Employees

Motivating and retaining employees is essential for the long-term success of your entrepreneurial venture. When your team members are motivated and engaged, they are more likely to perform at their best, contribute to the growth of your business, and stay committed to your organization. In this section, we will explore key strategies for motivating and retaining employees:

1. **Create a Positive Work Environment:** Foster a positive work environment where employees feel valued, respected, and supported. Encourage open communication, collaboration, and teamwork. Recognize and celebrate individual and team achievements. Promote a healthy work-life balance and prioritize employee well-being.

2. Provide Meaningful Work: Ensure that employees find their work meaningful and aligned with their skills, interests, and values. Help them understand how their contributions directly impact the success of the business and the fulfillment of its mission. Provide opportunities for employees to take on challenging projects and grow professionally.

3. Offer Competitive Compensation and Benefits: Provide competitive compensation packages that align with industry standards and the value employees bring to the organization. Additionally, offer attractive benefits such as health insurance, retirement plans, paid time off, and opportunities for professional development. Regularly review and update compensation and benefits to stay competitive.

4. Foster Career Growth and Development: Support the career growth and development of your employees. Offer opportunities for training, skill-building workshops, and mentorship programs. Provide clear paths for advancement and help employees set and achieve their career goals. Regularly discuss their aspirations and provide guidance on how they can progress within the organization.

5. Recognize and Reward Performance: Regularly recognize and reward employees for their exceptional performance and contributions. Implement a system of performance recognition that acknowledges individual and team achievements. This can include monetary rewards, public recognition, additional responsibilities, or career advancement opportunities.

6. Promote Work-Life Balance: Encourage and support work-life balance for your employees. Offer flexible working arrangements, such as flexible hours or remote work options, when feasible. Respect personal boundaries and encourage employees to take time off when needed. Promote a culture that values well-being and encourages self-care.

7. Foster a Culture of Feedback and Growth: Create a culture of continuous feedback and growth. Provide constructive feedback on a regular basis to help employees improve their performance. Encourage employees to share their ideas, concerns, and suggestions. Support their professional growth by providing learning opportunities and developmental feedback.

8. Encourage Autonomy and Ownership: Empower employees by giving them autonomy and ownership over their work. Provide them with the authority and resources needed to make decisions and accomplish their tasks. Encourage creativity, innovation, and entrepreneurial thinking. Trust employees to take ownership of their work and contribute to the success of the business.

9. Support Work Relationships and Team Building: Encourage strong work relationships and team building within your organization. Foster a sense of camaraderie and collaboration through team-building activities, off-site retreats, or social events. Promote cross-functional collaboration and create opportunities for employees to connect and build strong professional relationships.

10. Regularly Seek Feedback and Act on It: Regularly seek feedback from employees to understand their needs, concerns, and suggestions for improvement. Conduct employee surveys, one-on-one meetings, or anonymous suggestion boxes. Act on the feedback received and communicate the actions taken. Involve employees in decision-making processes when appropriate.

By implementing these strategies, you can create a motivating work environment and increase employee retention. Remember that each employee is unique, so it's important to tailor your approaches and recognize individual needs and aspirations. Regularly assess the effectiveness of your employee motivation and retention efforts and adapt your strategies as necessary to ensure long-term employee satisfaction and engagement.

Chapter 7
Developing a Marketing Strategy

Introduction

Developing a robust marketing strategy is essential for any entrepreneurial venture to attract and retain customers, build brand awareness, and drive business growth. In today's competitive landscape, having a well-defined marketing strategy is crucial for reaching your target market, effectively communicating your value proposition, and standing out from the competition. In this section, we will explore the key components of developing a successful marketing strategy:

1. **Understanding Your Target Market:** Begin by thoroughly understanding your target market. Identify the demographics, psychographics, and behavior patterns of your ideal customers. Conduct market research, analyze industry trends, and gather insights to gain a deep understanding of your target audience's needs, preferences, and pain points.

2. **Defining Your Value Proposition:** Clearly articulate your unique value proposition. Define what sets your product or service apart from competitors and how it addresses the specific needs of your target market. Identify the key benefits and advantages that differentiate your offering and communicate them effectively to your audience.

3. **Setting Marketing Objectives:** Establish clear marketing objectives that align with your overall business goals. These objectives could include increasing brand awareness, generating leads, driving sales,

or improving customer retention. Ensure that your objectives are specific, measurable, attainable, relevant, and time-bound (SMART).

4. Selecting Marketing Channels: Determine the most effective marketing channels to reach and engage your target audience. Consider a mix of online and offline channels, such as social media, content marketing, email marketing, search engine optimization (SEO), paid advertising, public relations, events, and partnerships. Tailor your channel selection based on your target market's preferences and behaviors.

5. Creating Compelling Content: Develop high-quality content that resonates with your target audience. Create informative blog posts, engaging videos, captivating social media posts, and valuable resources that address your audience's pain points and provide solutions. Craft content that showcases your expertise, builds trust, and establishes your brand as a thought leader in your industry.

6. Implementing Branding and Design: Develop a strong brand identity that reflects your unique value proposition and resonates with your target audience. Create a compelling logo, design consistent visual elements, and establish brand guidelines that ensure a cohesive and recognizable brand presence across all marketing materials and touchpoints.

7. Building Relationships through Engagement: Engage with your audience and build relationships through various channels. Respond to comments and messages on social media, host webinars or workshops, participate in industry events, and encourage customer reviews and testimonials. Foster a sense of community and build trust by actively engaging with your audience.

8. Tracking and Analyzing Results: Implement tracking and analytics tools to monitor the performance of your marketing efforts. Measure key metrics such as website traffic, conversions, email open rates,

social media engagement, and customer acquisition cost. Analyze the data to gain insights into the effectiveness of your marketing campaigns and make data-driven adjustments.

9. Iterating and Refining: Continuously iterate and refine your marketing strategy based on the insights gained from tracking and analyzing results. Stay up-to-date with industry trends and evolving customer preferences. Test new approaches, experiment with different channels, and optimize your marketing campaigns to achieve better results over time.

10. Staying Customer-Centric: Always keep your customers at the center of your marketing strategy. Listen to their feedback, understand their evolving needs, and adapt your marketing efforts accordingly. Continuously seek ways to enhance the customer experience, provide personalized messaging, and build long-term relationships with your customers.

Developing a comprehensive marketing strategy requires a deep understanding of your target market, a clear value proposition, and a thoughtful approach to selecting and implementing marketing channels. By following these key steps and continuously evaluating and refining your marketing efforts, you can create a marketing strategy that effectively promotes your entrepreneurial venture, engages your target audience, and drives business growth.

7.1 Defining Your Target Market

Defining your target market is a crucial step in developing an effective marketing strategy for your entrepreneurial venture. Your target market is the specific group of customers who are most likely to be interested in your product or service and are the primary focus of your marketing efforts. By understanding your target market, you can tailor your messaging, choose the right marketing channels, and deliver the right products or services that meet their needs. Here are some key steps to define your target market:

1. Conduct Market Research: Start by conducting thorough market research to gather data and insights about your industry, competitors, and potential customers. Analyze market trends, customer demographics, purchasing behavior, and any other relevant information that can help you understand the market landscape.

2. Identify Customer Demographics: Identify the demographic characteristics of your target market, such as age, gender, income level, education level, occupation, and geographic location. These factors can provide a basic understanding of who your potential customers are and help you tailor your marketing messages to resonate with them.

3. Segment Your Market: Divide your target market into segments based on common characteristics and behaviors. This segmentation can be done based on factors like lifestyle, interests, values, or specific needs. By segmenting your market, you can create more targeted marketing campaigns and address the unique preferences and pain points of each segment.

4. Analyze Customer Psychographics: Gain insights into the psychographics of your target market, which refers to their attitudes, beliefs, motivations, and lifestyle choices. Understand their values,

aspirations, challenges, and how they make purchasing decisions. This information will help you create marketing messages that resonate with their emotions and motivations.

5. Identify Pain Points and Needs: Identify the pain points, challenges, and needs that your target market faces. Determine how your product or service can provide a solution or fulfill their specific needs better than your competitors. Understanding these pain points will allow you to position your offering as the ideal solution for your target market.

6. Evaluate Competitor Positioning: Analyze how your competitors are positioning themselves in the market and who their target market is. Identify any gaps or underserved areas where you can differentiate yourself and cater to a specific niche within your target market. This will help you carve out a unique position for your venture.

7. Create Buyer Personas: Develop detailed buyer personas that represent your ideal customers within your target market. A buyer persona is a fictional representation of your target customer, including their demographics, behaviors, motivations, and goals. These personas help you understand your customers on a deeper level and guide your marketing efforts.

8. Validate and Refine: Continuously validate and refine your target market definition as you gather more information and data. Seek feedback from customers, conduct surveys or interviews, and monitor market trends to ensure that your understanding of your target market remains accurate and up to date.

Remember, defining your target market is an ongoing process. As your venture evolves and new opportunities arise, you may need to adjust your target market definition accordingly. Regularly evaluate the effectiveness of your marketing efforts and gather feedback from customers to ensure that you are effectively reaching and engaging your target market with your products or services.

7.2 Branding and Positioning

Branding and positioning are essential elements of a successful marketing strategy. Your brand is more than just a logo or a name; it encompasses the overall perception and reputation of your entrepreneurial venture in the minds of your target market. Positioning, on the other hand, is how you differentiate your venture from competitors and establish a unique place in the market. Effective branding and positioning strategies help you create a strong and memorable brand identity that resonates with your target audience. Here are key considerations for branding and positioning your venture:

1. Define Your Brand Identity: Start by defining your brand identity, which includes your brand values, mission, and personality. Think about what your venture stands for, what you want to be known for, and how you want your customers to perceive you. This will serve as the foundation for all your branding and positioning efforts.

2. Understand Your Target Market: Gain a deep understanding of your target market and their preferences, needs, and desires. This knowledge will help you tailor your brand messaging and positioning to resonate with your audience. Consider their demographics, psychographics, pain points, and aspirations when crafting your brand identity.

3. Develop a Compelling Brand Story: Craft a compelling brand story that engages your audience and communicates the unique value your venture offers. Your brand story should be authentic, memorable, and emotionally appealing. It should highlight your venture's origins, purpose, and the benefits it brings to customers.

4. Create a Distinctive Brand Name and Logo: Choose a brand name that is unique, memorable, and aligns with your brand identity. Design

a visually appealing and distinctive logo that represents your brand effectively. These elements will be the visual representation of your brand and will be featured across all marketing materials and touchpoints.

5. **Establish Brand Messaging:** Develop clear and consistent brand messaging that communicates your value proposition, key messages, and brand personality. Craft a tagline or a brand mantra that captures the essence of your venture. Ensure that your messaging resonates with your target market and sets you apart from competitors.

6. **Consistent Visual Branding:** Create a consistent visual branding strategy that includes color schemes, typography, and visual elements that reflect your brand identity. Use these consistently across all marketing channels, including your website, social media profiles, advertising materials, and packaging. Consistency helps to build recognition and reinforce your brand identity.

7. **Differentiate from Competitors:** Identify your unique selling points and how you differentiate yourself from competitors. Highlight the aspects of your venture that set you apart and provide value to your target market. This could be your product features, quality, customer service, or your brand values. Position yourself as the preferred choice within your target market.

8. **Deliver on Brand Promise:** Ensure that your venture consistently delivers on its brand promise. Consistency in delivering quality products or services, exceptional customer service, and upholding your brand values builds trust and loyalty among customers. Align your internal operations and culture with your brand identity to reinforce your brand promise.

9. **Engage and Connect with Your Audience:** Create opportunities to engage with your audience and build a strong connection. Leverage social media, content marketing, and other channels to interact with

your target market, listen to their feedback, and respond to their needs. Develop relationships that go beyond transactions and foster customer loyalty.

10. Evolve and Adapt: Continuously evaluate and refine your branding and positioning strategy as your venture grows and the market evolves. Stay updated with industry trends, monitor customer preferences, and be willing to adapt your brand strategy to remain relevant and meet the changing needs of your target market.

Effective branding and positioning create a strong and memorable identity for your venture, differentiate you from competitors, and build trust and loyalty among your target audience. By consistently delivering on your brand promise and engaging with your customers, you can establish a compelling brand presence that drives the success of your entrepreneurial venture.

7.3 Digital Marketing Strategies

In today's digital age, having a strong online presence is crucial for the success of your entrepreneurial venture. Digital marketing strategies enable you to reach a wider audience, engage with potential customers, and drive business growth. Here are key digital marketing strategies to consider:

1. Website Optimization: Your website serves as the foundation of your online presence. Optimize your website by ensuring it is visually appealing, user-friendly, and mobile-responsive. Implement search engine optimization (SEO) techniques to improve your website's visibility in search engine results and drive organic traffic.

2. Content Marketing: Develop a content marketing strategy to create and distribute valuable content that attracts and engages your target

audience. Create blog posts, videos, infographics, and other forms of content that address their pain points, provide solutions, and establish your expertise. Share your content through your website, blog, social media, and email newsletters.

3. Social Media Marketing: Leverage social media platforms to connect with your target audience, build brand awareness, and drive engagement. Identify the social media channels where your audience is most active and develop a social media marketing strategy. Create engaging content, interact with your audience, and use social media advertising to reach a wider audience.

4. Email Marketing: Build an email list of interested prospects and customers and use email marketing to nurture relationships and drive conversions. Develop a segmented email marketing strategy that delivers targeted and personalized content to different segments of your audience. Use email automation to streamline your campaigns and measure the effectiveness of your emails.

5. Search Engine Marketing (SEM): Implement paid search advertising campaigns, such as Google Ads, to appear in search engine results for relevant keywords. Use targeted keywords and ad copy to drive traffic to your website and generate leads. Continuously monitor and optimize your campaigns to maximize your return on investment (ROI).

6. Influencer Marketing: Collaborate with influencers or industry experts who have a significant following and influence over your target market. Partnering with influencers can help you reach a wider audience, build credibility, and generate brand awareness. Identify relevant influencers and establish mutually beneficial partnerships.

7. Video Marketing: Incorporate video marketing into your digital strategy to engage your audience effectively. Create informative and engaging videos that showcase your products, share valuable

insights, or provide tutorials. Share your videos on platforms like YouTube, social media, and your website to increase brand visibility.

8. Pay-Per-Click (PPC) Advertising: Utilize PPC advertising platforms, such as Google Ads or social media advertising, to display targeted ads to your audience. Set a budget, select specific targeting criteria, and create compelling ad campaigns that drive traffic and conversions. Monitor the performance of your ads and optimize them for better results.

9. Remarketing: Implement remarketing campaigns to re-engage with visitors who have previously interacted with your website or shown interest in your products or services. Use cookies to display targeted ads to these prospects as they browse other websites, reminding them of your brand and encouraging them to return and convert.

10. Analytics and Optimization: Regularly monitor and analyze the performance of your digital marketing efforts using analytics tools. Track key metrics such as website traffic, conversion rates, click-through rates, and social media engagement. Use this data to optimize your campaigns, refine your strategies, and improve your overall digital marketing ROI.

Remember, the digital marketing landscape is constantly evolving. Stay updated with the latest trends and technologies, adapt your strategies accordingly, and consistently evaluate the effectiveness of your digital marketing efforts. By leveraging the power of digital marketing, you can effectively reach and engage your target audience, drive brand awareness, and ultimately grow your entrepreneurial venture.

7.4 Measuring and Adjusting Marketing Efforts

Measuring and adjusting your marketing efforts is essential to ensure that your entrepreneurial venture is on track and achieving its marketing objectives. By tracking key performance indicators (KPIs) and analyzing data, you can gain valuable insights into the effectiveness of your marketing strategies and make informed adjustments to optimize your results. Here are some steps to effectively measure and adjust your marketing efforts:

1. Set Clear and Specific Goals: Start by setting clear and specific marketing goals that align with your overall business objectives. These goals could include increasing website traffic, improving conversion rates, generating leads, or boosting brand awareness. Having well-defined goals will help you measure the success of your marketing efforts.

2. Identify Key Performance Indicators (KPIs): Determine the KPIs that align with your marketing goals. These could include metrics such as website traffic, click-through rates, conversion rates, social media engagement, customer acquisition cost (CAC), or return on investment (ROI). Choose KPIs that provide meaningful insights into the performance of your marketing strategies.

3. Implement Tracking and Analytics: Use tracking tools and analytics platforms to monitor and measure the performance of your marketing campaigns. Install website analytics tools, such as Google Analytics, to track website traffic, user behavior, and conversion metrics. Utilize social media analytics to measure engagement, reach, and audience demographics. Set up conversion tracking to attribute leads or sales to specific marketing efforts.

4. Regularly Review and Analyze Data: Schedule regular reviews of your marketing data to assess the performance of your campaigns.

Analyze the collected data to identify trends, patterns, and areas of improvement. Look for insights on what is working well and what may need adjustment. Consider using data visualization tools to present the data in a visually appealing and easy-to-understand format.

5. Compare Results to Goals: Compare your actual results to the goals you set earlier. Determine if you are on track to meet your targets or if adjustments are needed. Analyze the gaps between actual performance and desired outcomes. This analysis will help you identify areas that require improvement or areas where you may need to allocate more resources.

6. Test and Experiment: Implement A/B testing or split testing to experiment with different marketing strategies or tactics. Test variations of your campaigns, such as different ad copy, visuals, or call-to-action buttons, to determine which performs better. Use the insights from these tests to refine your marketing approach and optimize your results.

7. Adjust Your Strategies: Based on the insights gained from data analysis and testing, make adjustments to your marketing strategies. This could involve reallocating your budget, targeting different customer segments, refining your messaging, or exploring new marketing channels. Continuously iterate and optimize your strategies to improve your marketing effectiveness.

8. Monitor Competitors: Keep an eye on your competitors' marketing efforts and strategies. Monitor their campaigns, messaging, and tactics to gain insights into what is working for them and how you can differentiate yourself. Use this information to adapt your own marketing strategies and stay competitive in the market.

9. Seek Customer Feedback: Regularly gather feedback from your customers through surveys, interviews, or social media listening. Understand their preferences, pain points, and perceptions of your

brand. Use this feedback to refine your marketing messaging, improve your customer experience, and enhance your overall marketing efforts.

10. Stay Updated and Evolve: Stay updated with the latest marketing trends, technologies, and consumer behaviors. Continuously educate yourself and your team on new marketing strategies, tools, and platforms. Be willing to adapt and evolve your marketing efforts to keep up with changing customer needs and market dynamics.

Remember that measuring and adjusting your marketing efforts is an ongoing process. Regularly track your KPIs, review your data, and make data-driven decisions to optimize your marketing strategies. By continuously improving and adapting your marketing efforts, you can maximize the impact of your entrepreneurial venture in the marketplace.

.

Part III:
Growing Your Business

Chapter 8
Sales and Customer Acquisition

Introduction

Sales and customer acquisition are essential aspects of any entrepreneurial venture. To achieve sustainable growth and profitability, you need to effectively sell your products or services and acquire new customers. This involves understanding your target market, developing sales strategies, and implementing customer acquisition tactics. In this section, we will explore various techniques and best practices for successful sales and customer acquisition. By mastering these skills, you can increase your revenue, expand your customer base, and drive the success of your venture.

In this chapter, we will cover the following topics:

1. Understanding Your Target Market: Before you can effectively sell to your customers, it is crucial to have a deep understanding of your target market. This involves identifying their needs, preferences, and pain points. By understanding their motivations and challenges, you can tailor your sales approach and value proposition to resonate with them.

2. Developing a Sales Strategy: A well-defined sales strategy provides a roadmap for achieving your sales goals. It includes setting objectives, identifying target customers, determining sales channels, and establishing key performance indicators. Your sales strategy should align with your overall business objectives and be adaptable to changing market conditions.

3. **Sales Techniques and Skills:** Mastering sales techniques and skills is vital for converting prospects into paying customers. This includes effective communication, active listening, objection handling, negotiation, and closing techniques. We will explore these techniques and provide practical tips for building rapport, demonstrating value, and overcoming objections.

4. **Building Customer Relationships:** Building strong and lasting customer relationships is crucial for long-term success. We will discuss strategies for cultivating customer loyalty, providing exceptional customer service, and maximizing customer satisfaction. By focusing on relationship-building, you can generate repeat business and benefit from positive word-of-mouth referrals.

5. **Lead Generation and Prospecting:** Acquiring new customers requires effective lead generation and prospecting strategies. We will explore different lead generation techniques, such as content marketing, social media marketing, email marketing, and networking. You will learn how to identify and qualify leads, nurture prospects, and convert them into customers.

6. **Effective Sales Presentations:** Delivering persuasive and compelling sales presentations is key to closing deals. We will discuss how to structure your presentations, deliver impactful messages, and showcase the value of your products or services. You will learn how to tailor your presentations to different audiences and effectively address their needs and concerns.

7. **Sales Metrics and Performance Tracking:** Monitoring and measuring your sales performance is essential for continuous improvement. We will explore key sales metrics, such as conversion rates, average deal size, and sales cycle length. You will learn how to track and analyze these metrics to identify areas for improvement and make data-driven decisions.

8. Sales Tools and Technology: Leveraging sales tools and technology can streamline your sales processes and enhance productivity. We will discuss customer relationship management (CRM) systems, sales automation tools, and other technologies that can support your sales efforts. You will learn how to leverage these tools to manage leads, track customer interactions, and optimize your sales workflow.

By mastering the art of sales and customer acquisition, you can drive revenue growth, expand your market presence, and build a strong foundation for the success of your entrepreneurial venture. In the following chapters, we will delve into each of these topics in more detail, providing practical guidance and actionable strategies to help you excel in sales and customer acquisition.

8.1 Building a Sales Pipeline

Building a sales pipeline is essential for maintaining a steady flow of potential customers and opportunities in your entrepreneurial venture. A sales pipeline represents the stages that a prospect goes through from initial contact to becoming a paying customer. By effectively managing your sales pipeline, you can prioritize leads, track progress, and increase your chances of closing deals. In this section, we will explore the key steps and best practices for building a robust sales pipeline.

1. Identify and Define Your Sales Stages: Start by identifying and defining the stages that a prospect typically goes through in your sales process. This could include stages such as lead generation, initial contact, qualification, proposal, negotiation, and closing. Each stage should have clear criteria and actions associated with it, enabling you to track progress and move prospects through the pipeline.

2. Qualify and Prioritize Leads: Not all leads are created equal. It is crucial to qualify leads based on their fit with your target market, level of interest, and potential to become a paying customer. Implement a lead qualification process that helps you determine which leads to prioritize and focus your efforts on. This will ensure that you allocate your time and resources effectively.

3. Generate Leads: To fill your sales pipeline, you need to generate a consistent flow of leads. Implement lead generation strategies such as content marketing, social media marketing, search engine optimization, and targeted advertising campaigns. Utilize various channels and tactics to attract potential customers and capture their interest.

4. Nurture Leads: Once you have identified potential leads, it is important to nurture them and build relationships. Develop a lead nurturing strategy that includes regular communication, providing relevant and valuable content, and addressing their specific needs and concerns. By staying top of mind and building trust, you can move leads closer to the conversion stage.

5. Track and Monitor Progress: Implement a system or CRM tool to track and monitor the progress of your leads through the sales pipeline. This will help you stay organized, identify bottlenecks, and prioritize your follow-ups. Regularly review your pipeline and assess the status of each lead to ensure that they are progressing smoothly.

6. Engage in Effective Communication: Communication is key throughout the sales pipeline. Engage in effective and timely communication with your leads, addressing their questions and concerns, providing relevant information, and maintaining regular touchpoints. Tailor your communication to the needs and preferences of each lead, utilizing various channels such as phone calls, emails, and meetings.

7. **Continuously Qualify and Requalify:** As leads move through the pipeline, continue to qualify and requalify them to ensure they are still a good fit for your offering. Circumstances may change, and it is important to assess if the lead's needs, budget, or timeline align with your product or service. This will help you focus your efforts on leads that have a higher probability of conversion.

8. **Provide Exceptional Customer Service:** Once a lead converts into a paying customer, the sales process doesn't end. Provide exceptional customer service to ensure customer satisfaction and promote loyalty. Delight your customers with personalized attention, prompt responses, and ongoing support. Happy customers are more likely to refer others and become advocates for your brand.

9. **Analyze and Optimize:** Regularly analyze your sales pipeline performance and identify areas for optimization. Review metrics such as conversion rates, sales cycle length, and pipeline velocity. Identify any bottlenecks or areas of improvement, and adjust your strategies and processes accordingly.

Building and managing a sales pipeline requires ongoing attention and effort. By implementing these best practices, you can ensure a steady flow of potential customers, effectively manage your leads, and increase your chances of closing deals. Remember to continuously evaluate and optimize your sales pipeline to align with the evolving needs of your target market and drive the success of your entrepreneurial venture.

8.2 Effective Sales Techniques

Mastering effective sales techniques is crucial for successfully selling your products or services and closing deals. The art of selling involves building rapport, understanding customer needs, addressing objections, and demonstrating the value of your offering. In this section, we will explore various sales techniques that can help you enhance your sales skills and improve your conversion rates. By incorporating these techniques into your sales approach, you can become a more persuasive and successful salesperson.

1. Active Listening: Effective salespeople are skilled listeners. Practice active listening by paying close attention to your prospects' needs, concerns, and desires. Ask open-ended questions to encourage them to share more information. By listening attentively, you can better understand their pain points and tailor your pitch to address their specific needs.

2. Building Rapport: Building rapport with your prospects is essential for establishing trust and creating a positive relationship. Find common ground, show genuine interest in their lives or businesses, and engage in friendly and meaningful conversations. This helps to create a comfortable and open environment that encourages prospects to share their thoughts and challenges.

3. Asking Probing Questions: Ask probing questions to dig deeper into your prospects' needs and motivations. These questions help you uncover their pain points, understand their goals, and identify how your product or service can provide value. Use open-ended questions that require more than a simple "yes" or "no" answer, allowing prospects to share their thoughts and provide valuable insights.

4. **Addressing Objections:** Prospects often have concerns or objections that prevent them from making a purchasing decision. Instead of avoiding or dismissing objections, address them directly. Understand the root cause of their objections and provide thoughtful and persuasive responses. Anticipate common objections in advance and prepare effective rebuttals to overcome them.

5. **Demonstrating Value:** Clearly articulate the unique value proposition of your product or service. Highlight the benefits and features that differentiate your offering from competitors. Use concrete examples and case studies to demonstrate how your product or service has solved similar problems for other customers. Show how your offering can bring tangible results and add value to your prospects' lives or businesses.

6. **Creating a Sense of Urgency:** Create a sense of urgency by emphasizing time-sensitive benefits or limited-time offers. Communicate the potential consequences of delaying a decision or highlight the value of taking immediate action. This can motivate prospects to make a purchasing decision sooner rather than later.

7. **Closing Techniques:** Closing a sale is the culmination of the sales process. Practice different closing techniques, such as the assumptive close, the choice close, or the trial close. Tailor your closing approach to the specific needs and preferences of your prospects. Be confident, ask for the sale, and guide prospects towards making a positive decision.

8. **Follow-Up and Persistence:** Effective salespeople understand the importance of follow-up and persistence. Even if a prospect doesn't convert immediately, maintain regular communication and continue to provide value. Stay top of mind by sending personalized follow-up emails, making phone calls, or scheduling meetings. Persistence can pay off when the timing is right for the prospect to make a purchasing decision.

9. **Continuous Learning and Improvement:** Sales techniques and strategies evolve over time. Stay updated with the latest sales trends, attend sales training workshops, read sales books, and learn from successful salespeople. Continuously improve your sales skills and adapt your approach to changing market dynamics and customer preferences.

Remember that effective sales techniques are built on a foundation of authenticity, empathy, and trust. Focus on building meaningful relationships, understanding your prospects' needs, and providing value. By incorporating these sales techniques into your approach, you can enhance your sales effectiveness and drive the success of your entrepreneurial venture.

8.3 Customer Relationship Management

Customer Relationship Management (CRM) is a strategic approach that focuses on building and maintaining strong relationships with your customers. It involves using technology, processes, and data to effectively manage interactions, track customer information, and provide personalized experiences. Implementing a CRM system can help you streamline your sales and marketing efforts, enhance customer satisfaction, and drive customer loyalty. In this section, we will explore the importance of CRM and how to effectively manage customer relationships.

1. **Benefits of CRM:** Implementing a CRM system offers several benefits for your entrepreneurial venture. It helps centralize customer data, allowing you to have a holistic view of each customer's interactions and history. This enables personalized communication and tailored marketing campaigns. CRM systems also facilitate

collaboration among teams, enhance customer service, improve sales forecasting, and provide valuable insights for decision-making.

2. Customer Data Management: Effective CRM begins with proper customer data management. Collect relevant customer information, such as contact details, preferences, purchase history, and interactions across various channels. Ensure data accuracy and consistency by implementing data validation processes and regularly updating customer records. A well-maintained CRM database serves as a single source of truth for customer information, enabling better understanding and engagement.

3. Segmentation and Personalization: Utilize CRM data to segment your customer base and create targeted marketing campaigns. By categorizing customers based on their characteristics, behaviors, and preferences, you can tailor your messages and offers to resonate with each segment. Leverage CRM tools to automate personalized communication, such as personalized emails, recommendations, and offers, fostering stronger customer relationships.

4. Sales and Lead Management: CRM systems assist in managing your sales pipeline and tracking leads throughout the sales process. Capture and store lead information, track their progress, and assign tasks to team members. This allows you to prioritize leads, ensure timely follow-ups, and maximize conversion rates. Use CRM reports and analytics to gain insights into your sales performance and identify areas for improvement.

5. Customer Service and Support: CRM systems facilitate effective customer service and support by providing a centralized platform for managing customer inquiries, complaints, and requests. Capture customer interactions, track service tickets, and ensure timely resolution of issues. Use CRM data to understand customer preferences and history, enabling personalized support and proactive engagement.

6. Cross-Selling and Upselling: CRM systems can help identify cross-selling and upselling opportunities with existing customers. By analyzing purchase history and customer behavior, you can identify complementary products or services to offer. Utilize CRM tools to automate personalized recommendations and targeted offers, increasing customer value and fostering loyalty.

7. Feedback and Surveys: CRM systems enable the collection of customer feedback and insights. Implement customer surveys, feedback forms, and ratings to gather valuable input on your products, services, and overall customer experience. Analyze this feedback to identify areas for improvement, address customer concerns, and make informed business decisions.

8. Integration with Marketing Automation: Integrate your CRM system with marketing automation tools to create seamless customer experiences. Automate marketing campaigns, lead nurturing, and personalized communications based on customer behavior and preferences. This integration allows for more efficient and effective marketing efforts, ultimately driving customer engagement and conversion.

9. Continuous Improvement: CRM is an ongoing process that requires continuous improvement. Regularly review and analyze CRM data, metrics, and reports to gain insights into customer behavior, sales performance, and customer satisfaction. Identify areas for improvement and adjust your strategies accordingly. Keep up with industry trends and advancements in CRM technology to leverage new opportunities.

Implementing a CRM system and adopting a customer-centric approach can significantly impact your entrepreneurial venture's success. By effectively managing customer relationships, you can enhance customer satisfaction, increase customer retention, and drive long-term business growth. Invest in CRM tools and practices that align with your business goals and customer needs, and continually strive to deliver exceptional customer experiences.

8.4 Scaling Your Sales Operations

Scaling your sales operations is a critical step in growing your entrepreneurial venture. It involves expanding your sales efforts to reach more customers, increase revenue, and achieve sustainable growth. However, scaling requires careful planning, effective strategies, and efficient processes. In this section, we will explore key considerations and best practices for scaling your sales operations successfully.

1. Assess Your Current Sales Processes: Before scaling, assess your existing sales processes to identify areas that need improvement or optimization. Review your lead generation, qualification, conversion, and customer retention strategies. Identify any bottlenecks, inefficiencies, or gaps that may hinder your scaling efforts. Streamline and optimize your processes to ensure scalability.

2. Define Your Target Market and Ideal Customer Profile: Clearly define your target market and ideal customer profile. Understand the characteristics, needs, and preferences of your ideal customers. This will help you focus your sales efforts on the right prospects and tailor your messaging and offerings accordingly. By targeting the right customers, you can optimize your sales resources and maximize your conversion rates.

3. Expand Your Sales Team: Scaling often requires expanding your sales team to handle increased demand and reach more customers. Assess your current team's capabilities and identify any skills gaps. Hire sales professionals who align with your company culture,

possess the necessary skills and experience, and can contribute to your growth goals. Provide proper training and support to help them succeed.

4. Implement Sales Enablement Tools: Sales enablement tools can greatly enhance your team's productivity and effectiveness. Consider implementing customer relationship management (CRM) systems, sales automation tools, and analytics platforms. These tools provide valuable insights, streamline processes, automate repetitive tasks, and improve collaboration among team members. Leverage technology to enable your sales team to scale efficiently.

5. Develop a Sales Playbook: Create a comprehensive sales playbook that outlines your sales process, key messaging, objection handling techniques, and best practices. This playbook serves as a reference guide for your sales team, ensuring consistency and alignment across your sales efforts. Update the playbook regularly to incorporate new learnings and strategies.

6. Invest in Sales Training and Development: Continuous training and development are essential for scaling your sales operations. Invest in sales training programs, workshops, and coaching to enhance your team's skills and knowledge. Provide ongoing support and mentorship to help your sales professionals adapt to changing market dynamics and refine their sales techniques.

7. Optimize Lead Generation Strategies: Scaling requires a consistent flow of high-quality leads. Evaluate your lead generation strategies and identify opportunities for improvement. Utilize a mix of inbound and outbound marketing tactics to reach your target audience effectively. Leverage digital marketing, content marketing, social media, and networking events to generate leads. Continuously test and refine your lead generation strategies to optimize results.

8. Implement Sales Forecasting and Analytics: Sales forecasting and analytics are crucial for making informed decisions and setting realistic goals. Utilize data and analytics to track and measure your sales performance, conversion rates, customer acquisition costs, and other key metrics. Leverage forecasting models to project future sales and identify potential bottlenecks or areas of opportunity. Data-driven insights will help you make strategic decisions and allocate resources effectively.

9. Foster a Culture of Accountability and Continuous Improvement: Scaling your sales operations requires a culture of accountability and continuous improvement. Set clear sales goals and targets, and hold your team accountable for achieving them. Regularly review and analyze sales performance, identify areas for improvement, and implement necessary changes. Encourage a growth mindset and a willingness to experiment and learn from failures.

10. Collaborate Across Departments: Scaling your sales operations is a cross-functional effort. Foster collaboration and communication between sales, marketing, customer service, and other relevant departments. Align your strategies and goals to ensure a seamless customer experience and maximize customer satisfaction. Encourage feedback and insights from different teams to drive innovation and growth.

Scaling your sales operations is an exciting yet challenging endeavor. By implementing effective strategies, optimizing processes, and investing in your sales team's development, you can successfully scale your sales operations and achieve sustainable growth for your entrepreneurial venture. Continuously evaluate and adapt your strategies as you scale, keeping customer satisfaction and long-term success in mind.

Chapter 9
Scaling and Expansion

Introduction

Scaling and expansion are critical stages in the growth journey of an entrepreneurial venture. They involve strategically increasing your operations, market presence, and customer base to achieve sustainable growth and maximize your business's potential. Scaling and expansion require careful planning, resource allocation, and execution. In this section, we will explore key considerations and strategies for successfully scaling and expanding your entrepreneurial venture.

1. Evaluating Growth Opportunities: Before embarking on the scaling and expansion journey, evaluate the potential growth opportunities available to your business. Assess market demand, competitive landscape, and customer preferences to identify areas where your products or services can thrive. Conduct thorough market research and analysis to ensure there is a viable market for your expansion efforts.

2. Strategic Planning: Develop a comprehensive strategic plan that outlines your objectives, targets, and the roadmap for scaling and expansion. Clearly define your vision, mission, and goals for the growth phase. Identify the resources, capabilities, and investments required to support your expansion efforts. Break down your plan into actionable steps and set realistic timelines for implementation.

3. Operational Efficiency: Streamline and optimize your operations to support scaling and expansion. Review your existing processes,

systems, and infrastructure to identify areas for improvement. Automate repetitive tasks, leverage technology solutions, and implement efficient workflows to increase productivity and reduce costs. Ensure scalability in your operations to accommodate the increased demand.

4. Financial Planning: Scaling and expansion often require significant financial resources. Develop a detailed financial plan that takes into account the costs associated with scaling, such as hiring new employees, marketing, infrastructure, and technology investments. Evaluate your funding options, including external financing, partnerships, or reinvesting profits. Seek professional advice if needed to ensure a solid financial foundation for your growth initiatives.

5. Talent Acquisition and Development: Scaling and expansion may require expanding your team or hiring new talent. Assess your current workforce and identify the skills and expertise needed to support your growth objectives. Develop a recruitment strategy to attract top talent who align with your company culture and possess the necessary skills to drive growth. Invest in employee training and development programs to enhance the capabilities of your team.

6. Market Expansion: Expanding your market reach is a key component of scaling and expansion. Identify new target markets, both geographically and demographically, where your products or services have potential demand. Develop tailored marketing and sales strategies to penetrate these markets effectively. Adapt your messaging, distribution channels, and pricing strategies to cater to the unique needs and preferences of the new markets.

7. Strategic Partnerships and Alliances: Explore strategic partnerships and alliances that can accelerate your scaling and expansion efforts. Collaborate with complementary businesses or industry influencers to gain access to new markets, leverage existing

customer bases, or enhance your product offerings. Seek mutually beneficial partnerships that align with your growth objectives and can provide strategic advantages.

8. Customer Experience and Retention: As you scale and expand, maintaining a positive customer experience becomes paramount. Focus on delivering exceptional customer service, ensuring product quality, and fostering strong customer relationships. Implement customer retention strategies to maximize customer lifetime value and drive customer loyalty. Leverage customer feedback and data to continuously improve your offerings and enhance the overall customer experience.

9. Monitor and Evaluate Performance: Regularly monitor and evaluate your performance during the scaling and expansion phase. Track key performance indicators (KPIs) and metrics to assess the effectiveness of your strategies and initiatives. Make data-driven decisions and adjust your approaches as needed. Continuously learn from your experiences, successes, and challenges to refine your growth strategies.

Scaling and expansion present exciting opportunities for your entrepreneurial venture, but they also come with their share of challenges. By carefully planning, strategically executing, and continuously adapting your strategies, you can successfully scale and expand your business, unlocking new levels of growth and success. Stay agile, innovative, and customer-focused throughout your scaling and expansion journey to ensure sustainable growth and long-term profitability.

9.1 Strategies for Growth

Scaling and expanding your entrepreneurial venture requires the implementation of effective growth strategies. These strategies are designed to propel your business forward, increase market share, and maximize profitability. In this section, we will explore various strategies that can help facilitate your growth and expansion efforts.

1. Market Penetration: Market penetration involves increasing your market share within your existing target market. This strategy focuses on capturing a larger portion of the market by attracting new customers or convincing existing customers to purchase more frequently. Utilize targeted marketing campaigns, pricing strategies, and customer loyalty programs to stimulate demand and gain a competitive edge.

2. Product Development: Product development strategies involve creating and launching new products or enhancing existing ones to meet the evolving needs and preferences of your target market. Conduct market research to identify gaps or opportunities for product innovation. Invest in research and development to create compelling offerings that differentiate your business from competitors and appeal to your customer base.

3. Market Expansion: Market expansion strategies involve entering new markets, either geographically or demographically. Identify untapped markets that align with your products or services and develop tailored marketing and distribution strategies to reach them. Conduct thorough market research to understand the unique characteristics, challenges, and opportunities of the new market and adapt your offerings accordingly.

4. Strategic Partnerships and Alliances: Collaborating with strategic partners can accelerate your growth and expansion efforts. Seek

partnerships with complementary businesses or industry leaders to leverage their resources, expertise, and customer base. Joint ventures, co-marketing initiatives, or distribution partnerships can provide access to new markets, enhance your brand visibility, and drive customer acquisition.

5. Franchising or Licensing: If your business model is easily replicable, consider franchising or licensing as a growth strategy. This allows you to expand your brand presence and reach through partnerships with independent franchisees or licensees. Ensure that you have robust systems, processes, and support mechanisms in place to maintain brand consistency and quality control.

6. Diversification: Diversification involves entering new markets or industries with new products or services that are different from your existing offerings. This strategy spreads risk and reduces dependence on a single market. Conduct thorough market research and assess the feasibility and potential profitability of diversifying into new areas. Carefully manage the transition and ensure that you have the necessary resources and expertise to enter the new market successfully.

7. Online Expansion and E-commerce: With the growing importance of digital channels, expanding your online presence and embracing e-commerce can open up new growth opportunities. Develop a robust online marketing strategy, optimize your website for search engines, and leverage social media platforms to reach and engage with a wider audience. Establish an e-commerce platform to enable online sales and tap into the global market.

8. Customer Retention and Upselling: While acquiring new customers is important, focusing on customer retention and upselling can contribute significantly to your growth. Implement customer retention strategies such as loyalty programs, personalized communication, and exceptional customer service. Upsell and cross-sell to existing

customers by offering complementary products or value-added services that meet their evolving needs.

9. International Expansion: If your business has the potential for global reach, consider expanding internationally. Conduct thorough market research to identify target countries with demand for your products or services. Adapt your offerings and marketing strategies to cater to the cultural, regulatory, and economic differences of the international markets. Establish local partnerships or set up international offices to support your expansion efforts.

10. Continuous Innovation and Adaptation: In a rapidly changing business environment, continuous innovation and adaptation are key to sustaining growth. Foster a culture of innovation within your organization, encourage employee creativity, and invest in research and development. Stay abreast of industry trends, emerging technologies, and evolving customer needs to identify new growth opportunities and stay ahead of the competition.

When implementing growth strategies, it is essential to monitor and evaluate their effectiveness through key performance indicators (KPIs) and adjust your approach as needed. Remember that successful growth requires careful planning, execution, and ongoing adaptation to ensure sustainable long-term success for your entrepreneurial venture.

9.2 Scaling Operations and Production

Scaling operations and production is a crucial aspect of growing and expanding your entrepreneurial venture. As your business experiences increased demand, it is essential to optimize your operations and production processes to meet the needs of a larger customer base. In this section, we will explore strategies and considerations for effectively scaling your operations and production.

1. Review and Streamline Processes: Start by reviewing your existing operational processes and identifying areas for improvement. Streamline workflows, eliminate bottlenecks, and automate repetitive tasks wherever possible. Look for opportunities to optimize efficiency and reduce costs without compromising quality.

2. Invest in Technology and Systems: Implementing the right technology and systems can significantly enhance your operational capabilities. Consider adopting enterprise resource planning (ERP) software to integrate and manage various aspects of your business, such as inventory management, production scheduling, and order fulfillment. Explore automation solutions, such as robotics or AI, to streamline production processes and improve efficiency.

3. Expand Facilities and Infrastructure: Scaling your operations often requires expanding your physical facilities and infrastructure. Assess your current space and equipment capacity to determine if additional resources are needed. Consider factors such as production capacity, storage space, and transportation logistics. If necessary, invest in larger facilities, machinery, or warehousing solutions to accommodate increased demand.

4. Supply Chain Optimization: Optimize your supply chain to ensure a smooth flow of materials and resources. Identify any potential bottlenecks or vulnerabilities in your supply chain and develop

strategies to mitigate risks. Strengthen relationships with suppliers and consider strategic partnerships to secure reliable and cost-effective sources of raw materials or components.

5. Workforce Management: Scaling operations may require hiring additional staff or upskilling existing employees. Assess your workforce needs and develop a hiring and training plan accordingly. Focus on recruiting individuals who align with your company culture and possess the skills and experience required to support your growing operations. Invest in employee training and development programs to enhance productivity and ensure consistency in quality.

6. Quality Control and Assurance: Maintaining consistent product quality is crucial as you scale your operations. Implement robust quality control measures and quality assurance processes to ensure that your products meet or exceed customer expectations. Conduct regular inspections, tests, and audits to identify and rectify any quality issues. Invest in training programs for your employees to maintain high-quality standards throughout the production process.

7. Collaboration and Communication: As your operations scale, effective collaboration and communication become even more critical. Foster a culture of collaboration within your organization, encouraging cross-functional teamwork and knowledge sharing. Implement communication channels, such as project management tools or collaboration software, to ensure smooth information flow and coordination among different departments.

8. Scalable Production Planning: Develop a scalable production plan that aligns with your growth objectives. Consider demand forecasting, production scheduling, and inventory management to optimize production efficiency and meet customer demands. Implement lean manufacturing principles, such as just-in-time inventory management, to minimize waste and maximize productivity.

9. Continuously Monitor and Optimize: Regularly monitor key performance indicators (KPIs) to track the performance of your operations and production processes. Analyze data to identify areas for improvement and make data-driven decisions. Implement a culture of continuous improvement, encouraging employees to provide feedback and suggestions for enhancing operational efficiency.

10. Flexibility and Adaptability: Finally, maintain flexibility and adaptability as you scale your operations. Recognize that scaling may require adjustments and refinements along the way. Be prepared to adapt your processes, systems, and strategies to meet changing market conditions and customer demands.

Scaling operations and production is a complex task that requires careful planning, resource allocation, and ongoing evaluation. By implementing these strategies and maintaining a focus on efficiency, quality, and adaptability, you can successfully scale your operations and meet the growing demands of your entrepreneurial venture.

9.3 Entering New Markets

Entering new markets is a key strategy for scaling and expanding your entrepreneurial venture. It allows you to tap into untapped customer segments, diversify your revenue streams, and increase your market presence. However, expanding into new markets requires careful planning, research, and execution. In this section, we will explore strategies and considerations for successfully entering new markets.

1. Market Research: Conduct thorough market research to identify potential target markets. Analyze market size, growth trends, competition, customer preferences, and regulatory requirements.

Understand the demographics, cultural nuances, and economic conditions of the new market to tailor your products or services effectively.

2. Customer Segmentation: Segment your target market based on demographics, psychographics, or other relevant criteria. Identify the specific customer segments that are most likely to be interested in your offerings in the new market. Develop a deep understanding of their needs, preferences, and purchasing behaviors to customize your marketing and sales strategies.

3. Competitive Analysis: Evaluate the competitive landscape in the new market. Identify key competitors, their market share, strengths, weaknesses, and market positioning. Understand how your offerings differentiate from competitors and develop strategies to highlight your unique value proposition.

4. Localization and Adaptation: Adapt your products, services, and marketing strategies to cater to the specific needs and preferences of the new market. Consider factors such as language, cultural norms, pricing, packaging, and branding. Localization may involve product modifications, language translation, or customization to align with local market expectations.

5. Distribution Channels: Determine the most effective distribution channels to reach your target customers in the new market. Evaluate options such as direct sales, partnerships with local distributors or retailers, e-commerce platforms, or franchising. Choose channels that align with your target market's shopping habits and ensure efficient product delivery.

6. Marketing and Promotion: Develop a targeted marketing and promotional strategy to create awareness and generate demand in the new market. Tailor your messaging, branding, and advertising campaigns to resonate with the local audience. Leverage digital

marketing channels, social media platforms, and local influencers to amplify your reach and engage with potential customers.

7. Strategic Partnerships: Consider forming strategic partnerships or alliances with local businesses or influencers to accelerate your market entry. Collaborate with established local companies to gain access to their customer base, distribution networks, or market knowledge. Partnering with influencers or opinion leaders can help build credibility and increase brand visibility.

8. Regulatory Compliance: Understand the regulatory environment and legal requirements of the new market. Ensure compliance with local laws, regulations, licensing, and certifications. Seek legal advice if needed to navigate any complexities or unique considerations in the new market.

9. Pilot Testing: Consider conducting a pilot test or soft launch in the new market before scaling up operations. This allows you to assess market response, gather feedback, and fine-tune your strategies. Use the pilot phase to identify any challenges or opportunities and make necessary adjustments before full-scale market entry.

10. Continuous Evaluation and Adaptation: Continuously monitor and evaluate your performance in the new market. Track key performance indicators (KPIs), customer feedback, and market trends. Adjust your strategies as needed to address market dynamics and changing customer needs. Stay agile and responsive to ensure long-term success in the new market.

Entering new markets is an exciting opportunity for growth, but it requires careful planning and execution. By conducting thorough market research, adapting to local needs, building strategic partnerships, and continuously evaluating your performance, you can successfully enter new markets and expand the reach of your entrepreneurial venture.

9.4 Managing Risk and Sustainability

As you scale and expand your entrepreneurial venture, it is essential to effectively manage risks and prioritize sustainability. Risk management helps protect your business from potential threats, while sustainability ensures the long-term viability and positive impact of your operations. In this section, we will explore strategies for managing risk and promoting sustainability in your entrepreneurial journey.

1. Risk Assessment and Mitigation: Conduct a comprehensive risk assessment to identify potential risks that could impact your business. This includes financial risks, operational risks, market risks, legal and regulatory risks, and external risks such as natural disasters or geopolitical events. Develop risk mitigation strategies and contingency plans to minimize the impact of potential risks.

2. Financial Risk Management: Maintain financial stability by implementing sound financial management practices. Monitor cash flow, budget effectively, and regularly review financial statements. Diversify your revenue streams and avoid excessive dependence on a single customer or market. Consider insurance coverage to protect against unforeseen events and liabilities.

3. Operational Risk Management: Identify and manage operational risks that can affect the efficiency and effectiveness of your business. This includes supply chain disruptions, equipment failures, cybersecurity threats, or human resource issues. Implement robust operational processes, quality control measures, and disaster recovery plans to mitigate operational risks.

4. Legal and Regulatory Compliance: Stay informed about relevant laws, regulations, and industry standards that apply to your business. Ensure compliance with legal requirements related to licensing,

permits, taxes, intellectual property, data privacy, and environmental regulations. Seek legal counsel when necessary to navigate complex compliance issues.

5. Sustainable Business Practices: Embrace sustainability as a core principle of your business. Integrate environmental, social, and governance (ESG) considerations into your decision-making processes. Implement sustainable practices such as energy efficiency, waste reduction, responsible sourcing, and ethical labor practices. Communicate your sustainability efforts transparently to stakeholders and customers.

6. Stakeholder Engagement: Build strong relationships with stakeholders, including employees, customers, suppliers, and the local community. Engage in open and transparent communication, actively seek feedback, and address concerns. Consider the social and environmental impact of your operations and collaborate with stakeholders to create shared value.

7. Crisis Management and Business Continuity: Develop a crisis management plan to effectively respond to emergencies or unexpected events. This includes communication protocols, alternative business arrangements, and contingency plans. Regularly review and update your plan to ensure its effectiveness in managing crises and maintaining business continuity.

8. Ethical Practices and Corporate Governance: Foster an ethical culture within your organization by promoting integrity, transparency, and accountability. Implement strong corporate governance practices and establish ethical guidelines for decision-making. This includes preventing conflicts of interest, ensuring fair and equal treatment of employees, and maintaining high ethical standards in your business dealings.

9. Continuous Learning and Improvement: Stay updated on emerging risks, sustainability trends, and best practices in risk management. Invest in employee training and development to enhance risk awareness and sustainability knowledge within your organization. Regularly review and evaluate your risk management and sustainability strategies to identify areas for improvement.

10. Collaboration and Partnerships: Collaborate with industry peers, organizations, and government agencies to share knowledge, resources, and best practices. Participate in sustainability initiatives and industry forums to contribute to collective efforts in managing risks and promoting sustainability. Leverage partnerships to address shared risks and drive positive change.

By effectively managing risk and prioritizing sustainability, you can enhance the resilience and long-term success of your entrepreneurial venture. Adopting a proactive and holistic approach to risk management and sustainability ensures that your business not only thrives but also contributes positively to society and the environment.

Chapter 10
Innovation and Adaptability

Introduction

Innovation and adaptability are key drivers of success in today's rapidly changing business landscape. As an entrepreneur, your ability to innovate, embrace new technologies, and adapt to evolving market conditions is crucial for staying competitive and seizing opportunities. In this section, we will explore the importance of innovation and adaptability and provide strategies to foster a culture of innovation and adaptability in your entrepreneurial journey.

Innovation drives growth and enables you to differentiate your products, services, and business model from competitors. It involves creating and implementing new ideas, processes, or solutions that add value to your customers and address their evolving needs. Innovation can take various forms, such as product innovation, process innovation, business model innovation, or even innovation in customer experience.

Adaptability, on the other hand, refers to your ability to respond and adjust to changing market dynamics, customer preferences, and technological advancements. It involves being agile, open to change, and proactive in identifying and seizing new opportunities. Being adaptable allows you to navigate uncertainties, overcome challenges, and stay relevant in a rapidly evolving business environment.

Creating a Culture of Innovation

Creating a culture of innovation starts with fostering an environment that encourages and rewards creativity, experimentation, and risk-taking. Here are some strategies to foster a culture of innovation in your entrepreneurial venture:

1. Encourage Idea Generation: Create channels and platforms for employees to share their ideas and suggestions. Foster an open and inclusive environment where everyone feels comfortable expressing their opinions and contributing to the innovation process.

2. Embrace Diversity: Embrace diversity in your workforce to bring together different perspectives, experiences, and expertise. Diverse teams are more likely to generate innovative ideas and challenge the status quo.

3. Provide Resources and Support: Allocate resources, such as time, funding, and tools, to support innovation initiatives. Create dedicated innovation teams or departments to focus on exploring new ideas and driving innovation within the organization.

4. Promote a Learning Culture: Encourage continuous learning and professional development among your employees. Support and provide opportunities for acquiring new skills, knowledge, and staying updated on industry trends and technological advancements.

5. Reward and Recognize Innovation: Establish a reward and recognition system that acknowledges and celebrates innovative ideas and contributions. This can include monetary incentives, public recognition, or career advancement opportunities.

6. Encourage Collaboration: Foster a collaborative environment where employees from different departments or disciplines can collaborate

on innovative projects. Encourage cross-functional teamwork and create platforms for sharing knowledge and ideas.

7. Embrace Failure as a Learning Opportunity: Encourage a mindset where failure is seen as a stepping stone to learning and improvement. Create a safe space where employees feel comfortable taking calculated risks and learning from setbacks.

Embracing Adaptability

Embracing adaptability is crucial for staying ahead in a dynamic business environment. Here are strategies to foster adaptability in your entrepreneurial venture:

1. Stay Informed: Stay updated on industry trends, market changes, and emerging technologies that may impact your business. Regularly conduct market research and competitive analysis to identify new opportunities and threats.

2. Foster a Growth Mindset: Cultivate a growth mindset among your employees, encouraging them to embrace change, learn from failures, and continuously improve. Encourage a willingness to learn new skills, adapt to new technologies, and explore new ideas.

3. Encourage Flexibility: Foster a flexible work environment that allows for agile decision-making and adaptation. Encourage employees to be open to change, explore new approaches, and adapt their strategies based on feedback and market conditions.

4. Seek Customer Feedback: Actively seek feedback from your customers to understand their changing needs, preferences, and pain points. Use customer insights to adapt your products, services, and customer experience accordingly.

5. Foster Collaboration and Cross-Functional Communication:

Encourage collaboration and communication across different teams and departments within your organization. This helps break silos and enables a more holistic and adaptable approach to problem-solving.

6. **Develop a Network of Strategic Partnerships:** Build strategic partnerships with other businesses or organizations that complement your offerings. Collaborate with partners to leverage their expertise, resources, and networks to adapt and seize new opportunities.

7. Embrace Technology: Embrace new technologies and digital tools that can enhance your business operations, improve efficiency, and enable you to adapt to changing market demands. Stay informed about emerging technologies relevant to your industry and explore how they can be leveraged to gain a competitive edge.

Innovation and adaptability are essential for entrepreneurial success. By fostering a culture of innovation, embracing adaptability, and continuously seeking new opportunities, you can position your entrepreneurial venture for long-term growth and relevance in a rapidly changing business landscape.

10.1 Embracing Change and Disruption

Change and disruption are inevitable in today's fast-paced and dynamic business environment. As an entrepreneur, your ability to embrace change and navigate disruptions effectively can determine the success and longevity of your venture. In this section, we will explore the importance of embracing change and disruption and provide strategies to thrive amidst constant shifts in the business landscape.

1. Embrace a Growth Mindset: Adopt a growth mindset that sees change and disruption as opportunities for learning, growth, and innovation. Embrace challenges and setbacks as learning experiences that can propel you forward. Cultivate a mindset of curiosity, adaptability, and resilience.

2. Stay Agile and Flexible: Build agility and flexibility into your business operations and decision-making processes. Be willing to adapt and adjust your strategies, products, and services in response to changing market conditions and customer demands. Emphasize speed and nimbleness in your organizational culture.

3. Continuously Monitor the Business Landscape: Stay informed about industry trends, technological advancements, and market shifts. Monitor changes in customer behavior, preferences, and needs. Regularly conduct market research and competitor analysis to identify emerging opportunities and potential threats.

4. Foster Innovation and Experimentation: Encourage a culture of innovation and experimentation within your organization. Create an environment where new ideas are welcomed, and employees are empowered to take calculated risks. Allocate resources for research and development, and provide opportunities for employees to explore innovative solutions.

5. Build Strategic Partnerships: Collaborate with other businesses, organizations, and industry experts to navigate disruptions and leverage new opportunities. Strategic partnerships can provide access to complementary resources, expertise, and networks that can help you adapt and thrive in the face of change.

6. Develop a Plan for Change Management: Anticipate potential disruptions and develop a comprehensive plan for change management. Identify potential risks and challenges associated with change, and create strategies to mitigate them. Communicate transparently with stakeholders and involve them in the change process to build support and alignment.

7. Invest in Continuous Learning and Skill Development: Stay ahead of the curve by investing in continuous learning and skill development for yourself and your team. Develop a culture of ongoing education and provide opportunities for training, workshops, and professional development. Encourage employees to acquire new skills and knowledge to adapt to changing business needs.

8. Foster a Resilient Organizational Culture: Build a resilient organizational culture that encourages adaptability and perseverance. Foster open communication, collaboration, and trust within your team. Celebrate successes and learn from failures. Provide support and resources for employees to navigate change and maintain morale.

9. Anticipate and Prepare for Disruptions: Develop contingency plans and risk management strategies to prepare for potential disruptions. Assess potential risks and vulnerabilities in your business, and create strategies to mitigate them. Diversify your revenue streams and customer base to reduce dependence on specific markets or segments.

10. Embrace Technology and Digital Transformation: Embrace technological advancements and digital transformation to stay competitive and agile. Leverage technology to streamline operations, enhance customer experiences, and explore new business models. Stay informed about emerging technologies relevant to your industry and proactively integrate them into your strategies.

By embracing change and disruption, you position yourself and your entrepreneurial venture to thrive in an ever-evolving business landscape. Embrace the opportunities that arise from change, cultivate an agile mindset, and build strategies to adapt and innovate. Remember, change is not a threat but a catalyst for growth and success.

10.2 Fostering Innovation in Your Business

Innovation is a vital driver of growth, competitiveness, and long-term success for businesses. Fostering a culture of innovation within your entrepreneurial venture can unlock new opportunities, drive creativity, and help you stay ahead of the curve. In this section, we will explore strategies to foster innovation within your business.

1. Encourage Idea Generation: Create an environment where ideas are encouraged and welcomed from all levels of the organization. Establish channels for employees to share their ideas, suggestions, and feedback. Foster an open and inclusive culture that values and rewards creativity and innovation.

2. Promote a Learning Mindset: Cultivate a learning mindset within your organization by encouraging employees to pursue continuous learning and development. Provide opportunities for training, workshops, and conferences that expose employees to new ideas, skills, and perspectives.

3. Embrace Diversity: Build a diverse workforce that encompasses a range of backgrounds, experiences, and perspectives. Diversity brings a wealth of ideas and fresh insights, fostering innovation through different viewpoints and approaches. Create an inclusive environment where diverse voices are heard and valued.

4. Establish Innovation Teams or Committees: Dedicate resources and create dedicated teams or committees focused on driving innovation within your organization. Empower these teams to explore new ideas, conduct experiments, and develop innovative solutions. Provide them with the necessary support and resources to bring their ideas to life.

5. Reward and Recognize Innovation: Implement a reward and recognition system that acknowledges and celebrates innovative ideas and contributions. Provide incentives, such as bonuses, promotions, or public recognition, to individuals or teams that generate and implement successful innovations. This reinforces the value placed on innovation within the organization.

6. Foster Collaboration and Cross-functional Teams: Encourage collaboration and teamwork across different departments and functions. Foster a culture where employees from diverse backgrounds come together to solve problems and share ideas. Cross-functional teams can bring together diverse skills and knowledge, leading to more innovative solutions.

7. Provide Resources and Support: Allocate resources, such as time, funding, and tools, to support innovation initiatives. Establish innovation labs or dedicated spaces for experimentation and idea development. Provide access to technology, research materials, and external expertise to facilitate the innovation process.

8. **Encourage Risk-Taking:** Create a safe environment where employees feel empowered to take calculated risks and experiment with new ideas. Encourage learning from failures and provide support for employees to bounce back from setbacks. Instill a culture where taking risks is seen as a necessary step towards innovation and growth.

9. **Stay Connected to Customers and Market Trends:** Regularly engage with customers to understand their evolving needs, preferences, and pain points. Monitor market trends, emerging technologies, and industry disruptions. Use customer insights and market intelligence to drive innovation efforts and develop solutions that address real-world problems.

10. **Foster an Entrepreneurial Mindset:** Encourage employees to think like entrepreneurs and take ownership of their work. Foster an entrepreneurial mindset that encourages creative problem-solving, initiative, and a willingness to challenge the status quo. Provide autonomy and freedom to employees to explore and implement their ideas.

By implementing these strategies, you can create a culture of innovation that permeates throughout your organization. Fostering innovation will enable your entrepreneurial venture to adapt to changing market dynamics, identify new opportunities, and deliver unique value to your customers. Embrace innovation as a core element of your business strategy and empower your team to drive meaningful change.

10.3 Adapting to Industry Trends

Adapting to industry trends is crucial for the success and sustainability of your entrepreneurial venture. As markets evolve, customer preferences change, and new technologies emerge, it is essential to stay abreast of industry trends and proactively adjust your business strategies. In this section, we will explore strategies to effectively adapt to industry trends.

1. Continuous Market Research: Conduct regular market research to identify emerging trends, consumer behavior shifts, and market dynamics. Stay informed about industry reports, market studies, and customer surveys. Analyze market data to uncover opportunities and potential threats that may arise from industry trends.

2. Monitor Competitors: Keep a close eye on your competitors and analyze their strategies, product offerings, and customer engagement approaches. Identify areas where they are successfully adapting to industry trends and learn from their practices. Differentiate your business by identifying gaps and offering unique value propositions.

3. Embrace Technological Advancements: Stay updated on technological advancements relevant to your industry. Embrace new technologies that can improve operational efficiency, enhance customer experiences, or open up new avenues for growth. Experiment with emerging technologies and evaluate their potential impact on your business.

4. Foster Innovation and Experimentation: Create a culture of innovation that encourages experimentation and the exploration of new ideas. Allocate resources and time for innovation initiatives within your organization. Encourage employees to propose and test innovative solutions that align with industry trends.

5. Stay Connected with Customers: Regularly engage with your customers to understand their evolving needs, preferences, and pain points. Utilize feedback channels, conduct surveys, and maintain active social media presence to stay connected with your target audience. Use customer insights to adapt your products, services, and marketing strategies.

6. Build Strategic Partnerships: Collaborate with industry partners, suppliers, and distributors to leverage their expertise and adapt to industry trends. Seek out strategic partnerships that can help you access new markets, expand your customer base, or gain insights into emerging trends. Joint ventures or alliances can provide opportunities for shared learning and mutual growth.

7. Invest in Employee Development: Equip your employees with the necessary skills and knowledge to adapt to industry trends. Provide training and development programs to keep them updated on the latest industry practices and technologies. Encourage a culture of continuous learning and professional growth within your organization.

8. Be Agile and Flexible: Build flexibility into your business processes and decision-making. Be prepared to adjust your strategies, product offerings, and operational approaches in response to industry trends. Embrace an agile mindset that allows for quick adaptation and experimentation.

9. Seek External Expertise: Consult industry experts, advisors, or consultants who specialize in your field. Seek their guidance and insights on industry trends and best practices. Engage in industry associations, attend conferences, and participate in networking events to stay connected with the broader industry ecosystem.

10. Monitor Regulatory and Policy Changes: Stay informed about regulatory and policy changes that may impact your industry.

Anticipate potential shifts in regulations or compliance requirements and proactively adapt your business practices accordingly.

By actively monitoring and adapting to industry trends, you can position your entrepreneurial venture for long-term success. Embrace change, leverage emerging technologies, and foster a culture of innovation and agility. Continuously evaluate and adjust your strategies to align with industry trends and meet the evolving needs of your customers.

10.4 Staying Ahead of the Competition

In today's competitive business landscape, it is crucial for entrepreneurs to stay ahead of the competition to sustain and grow their ventures. By constantly assessing market dynamics, understanding customer needs, and strategically positioning your business, you can gain a competitive edge. In this section, we will explore strategies to stay ahead of the competition.

1. Conduct Competitor Analysis: Regularly analyze your competitors to gain insights into their strategies, strengths, weaknesses, and market positioning. Identify what sets you apart and develop strategies to differentiate your products or services. Monitor their pricing, marketing tactics, and customer experiences to identify areas where you can excel.

2. Focus on Unique Value Proposition: Clearly define and communicate your unique value proposition to customers. Identify what makes your products or services different and better than competitors. Emphasize your unique features, benefits, or customer experience to stand out in the market.

3. **Anticipate Customer Needs:** Stay attuned to changing customer needs and preferences. Conduct market research, gather customer feedback, and monitor industry trends to understand evolving demands. Proactively adapt your products, services, and marketing strategies to meet and exceed customer expectations.

4. **Foster Innovation:** Embrace a culture of innovation within your organization. Encourage employees to generate new ideas, explore creative solutions, and challenge the status quo. Foster an environment that rewards innovation and supports the implementation of novel approaches. Continuously improve your products, processes, and customer experiences to stay ahead.

5. **Embrace Technology:** Leverage technology to streamline operations, enhance efficiency, and deliver superior customer experiences. Stay informed about technological advancements relevant to your industry. Embrace digital transformation, automation, and data analytics to gain a competitive advantage. Utilize technology to innovate and differentiate your offerings.

6. **Build Strong Customer Relationships:** Focus on building strong relationships with your customers. Provide excellent customer service, actively listen to their feedback, and personalize their experiences. Foster loyalty and repeat business by delivering exceptional value and exceeding their expectations. Establish a strong brand reputation based on trust and customer satisfaction.

7. **Stay Agile and Adaptable:** Be responsive to changing market conditions and customer needs. Remain flexible and willing to adjust your strategies, products, or services as required. Embrace an agile mindset that allows you to seize opportunities and navigate challenges swiftly. Adapt your business to stay relevant and competitive.

8. Invest in Marketing and Branding: Develop effective marketing strategies to promote your business and differentiate yourself from competitors. Invest in branding initiatives that convey your unique value proposition and build brand recognition. Utilize various marketing channels, including digital marketing, social media, and content marketing, to reach and engage your target audience.

9. Develop Strategic Partnerships: Collaborate with strategic partners to leverage their expertise, resources, and networks. Seek partnerships that can expand your reach, access new markets, or enhance your product offerings. Joint ventures, alliances, or strategic alliances can provide a competitive advantage through shared knowledge and combined strengths.

10. Continuous Learning and Improvement: Foster a culture of continuous learning and improvement within your organization. Encourage employees to enhance their skills and stay updated on industry trends. Invest in professional development opportunities, training programs, and knowledge-sharing platforms. Continuously evaluate and improve your business processes to enhance efficiency and effectiveness.

By implementing these strategies, you can position your entrepreneurial venture to outperform competitors and thrive in the market. Stay focused on delivering value, understanding customer needs, and continuously innovating. Monitor the competitive landscape, adapt to changes, and invest in strategies that differentiate your business. Remember, staying ahead of the competition is an ongoing process that requires continuous effort and a commitment to excellence.

Part IV:
Sustaining Success

Chapter 11
Financial Management and Planning

Introduction

Financial management and planning are crucial elements for the success and sustainability of any entrepreneurial venture. Effective financial management ensures that resources are allocated efficiently, risks are mitigated, and profitability is maximized. In this section, we will explore the key principles and strategies of financial management and planning for entrepreneurs.

1. Understanding Financial Statements: Gain a solid understanding of financial statements, including the balance sheet, income statement, and cash flow statement. These statements provide insights into your company's financial health, profitability, and cash flow. Regularly review and analyze financial statements to track performance, identify trends, and make informed financial decisions.

2. Budgeting and Forecasting: Develop a comprehensive budget and financial forecast that outlines your revenue and expense projections for a specific period. Budgeting helps you allocate resources effectively, set financial goals, and monitor actual performance against planned targets. Regularly review and adjust your budget as needed to adapt to changing circumstances.

3. Managing Cash Flow: Cash flow management is crucial for the day-to-day operations of your business. Monitor your cash inflows and outflows to ensure that you have sufficient liquidity to meet your financial obligations. Implement strategies to improve cash flow, such

as optimizing your payment terms, managing inventory levels, and controlling expenses.

4. Cost Control and Expense Management: Analyze your expenses and identify areas where you can reduce costs without compromising quality or operational efficiency. Implement cost control measures such as negotiating better supplier contracts, optimizing inventory management, and eliminating unnecessary expenses. Regularly review your cost structure to identify potential savings opportunities.

5. Pricing Strategies: Develop a pricing strategy that aligns with your business goals and market dynamics. Consider factors such as production costs, competitor pricing, and customer value. Ensure that your pricing strategy allows for a sustainable profit margin while remaining competitive in the market.

6. Financial Risk Management: Identify and assess financial risks that may impact your business. Implement risk management strategies such as diversifying revenue streams, creating contingency plans, and obtaining appropriate insurance coverage. Regularly monitor and mitigate financial risks to protect your business from potential disruptions.

7. Capital Structure and Financing Options: Evaluate your capital structure and financing needs. Determine the optimal mix of debt and equity financing that aligns with your growth objectives and risk tolerance. Explore financing options such as loans, grants, venture capital, or crowdfunding, and carefully consider their implications on your financial health and ownership structure.

8. Financial Analysis and Performance Metrics: Utilize financial analysis tools and performance metrics to evaluate the financial performance of your business. Key metrics may include profitability ratios, liquidity ratios, and efficiency ratios. Regularly assess your

financial performance to identify areas for improvement and make data-driven decisions.

9. Tax Planning and Compliance: Understand the tax implications of your business activities and develop a tax planning strategy to optimize your tax obligations. Ensure compliance with relevant tax laws and regulations, and consider seeking professional advice to navigate complex tax issues.

10. Seek Professional Financial Advice: Consider consulting with financial professionals, such as accountants or financial advisors, to gain expert insights and guidance. They can help you navigate complex financial matters, provide objective analysis, and assist in making informed financial decisions.

Effective financial management and planning are essential for the long-term success of your entrepreneurial venture. By implementing sound financial practices, you can make informed decisions, manage risks, and optimize financial performance. Regularly review and adjust your financial strategies to adapt to changing market conditions and achieve your business goals.

11.1 Understanding Financial Statements

Financial statements provide a comprehensive overview of a company's financial performance and position. They are essential tools for entrepreneurs to assess the health of their business, make informed decisions, and communicate financial information to stakeholders. In this section, we will delve into the key components and principles of understanding financial statements.

1. The Balance Sheet: The balance sheet, also known as the statement of financial position, provides a snapshot of a company's

financial position at a specific point in time. It presents the company's assets, liabilities, and shareholders' equity. The balance sheet follows the fundamental equation: Assets = Liabilities + Shareholders' Equity. It helps entrepreneurs understand the company's net worth and the composition of its assets and liabilities.

2. The Income Statement: The income statement, also known as the statement of profit and loss or statement of operations, presents the company's revenue, expenses, and net income over a specific period. It showcases the company's ability to generate profit from its operations. The income statement follows the equation: Revenue - Expenses = Net Income. Entrepreneurs can analyze the income statement to evaluate revenue trends, cost structures, and overall profitability.

3. The Cash Flow Statement: The cash flow statement tracks the flow of cash in and out of the company over a specific period. It categorizes cash flows into three main sections: operating activities, investing activities, and financing activities. The cash flow statement provides insights into a company's liquidity, its ability to generate cash from operations, and its cash flow management. Entrepreneurs can assess the company's cash position and evaluate its cash flow generation and usage.

4. Financial Ratios: Financial ratios are tools used to analyze the relationships between different elements of financial statements. They help entrepreneurs assess various aspects of a company's financial performance, including profitability, liquidity, solvency, and efficiency. Common financial ratios include the gross profit margin, current ratio, debt-to-equity ratio, and return on investment. By calculating and interpreting these ratios, entrepreneurs can gain insights into the financial health and performance of their business.

5. Notes to the Financial Statements: The notes to the financial statements provide additional details, explanations, and disclosures

related to the information presented in the financial statements. They include important accounting policies, significant events, contingent liabilities, and other relevant information. Entrepreneurs should review the notes to gain a deeper understanding of the financial statements and the specific circumstances affecting the company's financial position and performance.

6. Accounting Principles and Standards: Financial statements are prepared in accordance with generally accepted accounting principles (GAAP) or international financial reporting standards (IFRS), depending on the jurisdiction. These principles and standards provide guidelines for recording and reporting financial information. Entrepreneurs should familiarize themselves with the applicable accounting principles to ensure accurate and reliable financial statements.

7. Using Financial Statements for Decision-Making: Entrepreneurs can utilize financial statements to make informed decisions about their business. By analyzing trends, comparing financial ratios, and conducting financial statement analysis, entrepreneurs can identify areas of strength and weakness, assess the impact of business decisions, and develop strategies for improvement. Financial statements serve as a basis for financial forecasting, budgeting, and setting performance targets.

It is essential for entrepreneurs to understand and interpret financial statements accurately to make sound financial decisions. By gaining proficiency in analyzing financial statements, entrepreneurs can effectively manage their company's financial performance, communicate with stakeholders, and drive sustainable growth.

11.2 Budgeting and Cash Flow Management

Budgeting and cash flow management are critical components of financial planning for entrepreneurs. Effective budgeting allows entrepreneurs to allocate resources wisely, set financial goals, and track performance. Cash flow management ensures that a company has sufficient liquidity to meet its financial obligations and sustain its operations. In this section, we will explore the principles and strategies of budgeting and cash flow management for entrepreneurial ventures.

1. Developing a Budget: Start by creating a comprehensive budget that outlines your projected revenue and expenses for a specific period, typically on a monthly or annual basis. Consider all sources of revenue, such as sales, investments, or loans, and categorize your expenses into fixed costs (e.g., rent, salaries) and variable costs (e.g., raw materials, marketing). Your budget should also include provisions for taxes, contingencies, and capital expenditures.

2. Setting Financial Goals: Align your budget with your business goals and objectives. Define specific financial targets, such as revenue growth, profitability ratios, or cash flow targets. Setting measurable goals helps you track progress, make informed decisions, and take corrective actions if needed.

3. Monitoring and Reviewing Actual Performance: Regularly compare your actual financial performance against the budgeted amounts. Monitor key financial metrics, such as revenue, expenses, gross margin, and net profit. Identify any significant variances and investigate the underlying causes. This allows you to take proactive measures to address issues, capitalize on opportunities, and make adjustments to your budget if necessary.

4. **Controlling Expenses:** Review your expenses regularly and identify areas where cost savings can be achieved without sacrificing quality or operational efficiency. Consider negotiating better terms with suppliers, optimizing your inventory management, or implementing cost-cutting measures. By controlling expenses, you can improve profitability and enhance your cash flow.

5. **Cash Flow Forecasting:** Develop a cash flow forecast that projects the inflows and outflows of cash for a specific period. It helps you anticipate periods of cash surplus or shortage and plan accordingly. Consider factors such as customer payment terms, supplier payment terms, inventory turnover, and seasonal variations in sales. A cash flow forecast enables you to take proactive steps to manage cash flow effectively.

6. **Managing Accounts Receivable:** Implement robust accounts receivable management practices to ensure timely collection of payments from customers. Establish clear credit terms, send timely and accurate invoices, and follow up on overdue payments. Consider offering incentives for early payments and enforce collection policies when necessary. Efficient accounts receivable management helps maintain a healthy cash flow.

7. **Optimizing Accounts Payable:** Work closely with suppliers to negotiate favorable payment terms. Maximize the credit period available to you while maintaining good relationships with your suppliers. However, ensure that you honor your payment commitments promptly to preserve supplier relationships and maintain a reliable supply chain.

8. **Working Capital Management:** Pay attention to your working capital, which represents the difference between current assets and current liabilities. Efficient working capital management ensures that you have enough liquidity to meet short-term obligations. Evaluate your inventory levels, manage accounts payable and receivable, and

optimize your cash conversion cycle. By effectively managing working capital, you can improve cash flow and overall financial stability.

9. Cash Flow Buffer: Establish a cash flow buffer to account for unforeseen events or temporary cash flow gaps. This buffer provides a safety net to cover unexpected expenses or revenue fluctuations. Maintain a reserve of cash or access to a line of credit that can be utilized during challenging times.

10. Seeking Professional Advice: Consider engaging financial professionals, such as accountants or financial advisors, to assist you in budgeting and cash flow management. They can provide expertise, guidance, and help in developing realistic budgets, cash flow forecasts, and strategies for managing your financial resources effectively.

Effective budgeting and cash flow management are essential for the financial health and sustainability of

your entrepreneurial venture. By developing accurate budgets, monitoring performance, and implementing robust cash flow management practices, you can make informed decisions, navigate financial challenges, and ensure the long-term success of your business.

11.3 Financial Decision-Making

Financial decision-making is a critical aspect of entrepreneurship that involves evaluating various options, weighing risks and rewards, and making informed choices to maximize the financial performance and value of a business. In this section, we will explore key principles and strategies for effective financial decision-making in the entrepreneurial context.

1. Investment Decisions: When considering investment opportunities, entrepreneurs must assess the potential returns and risks associated with each option. Conduct a thorough analysis of the expected cash flows, payback period, internal rate of return (IRR), and net present value (NPV) of the investments. Consider factors such as market conditions, competitive landscape, and your business's strategic objectives before making investment decisions.

2. Financing Decisions: Entrepreneurs often face the challenge of determining the best financing options for their ventures. Evaluate various sources of financing, such as equity investments, loans, grants, or crowdfunding. Consider the costs, terms, and conditions associated with each option, as well as the impact on ownership, control, and future financial obligations. Assess the optimal capital structure that balances the need for capital with the risk tolerance and financial health of the business.

3. Capital Budgeting: Capital budgeting involves allocating financial resources to specific projects or investments within the business. Apply techniques such as discounted cash flow (DCF) analysis, net present value (NPV), and internal rate of return (IRR) to evaluate the feasibility and profitability of potential projects. Prioritize investments based on their potential return on investment (ROI) and alignment with the company's strategic goals.

4. Risk Management: Financial decision-making should involve a thorough assessment of risks and the implementation of risk management strategies. Identify and quantify risks associated with investments, financing, cash flow, market conditions, competition, and regulatory changes. Develop contingency plans, diversify risk exposure, and consider insurance coverage to mitigate potential risks. Regularly monitor and review risk factors to make informed decisions that balance risk and reward.

5. Cost-Volume-Profit Analysis: Cost-volume-profit (CVP) analysis helps entrepreneurs understand the relationship between costs, volume, pricing, and profit. It helps determine the breakeven point, assess the impact of pricing decisions on profitability, and analyze the effects of changes in sales volume. Use CVP analysis to make pricing decisions, set sales targets, and evaluate the financial viability of different business models or product lines.

6. Financial Forecasting and Scenario Analysis: Develop financial forecasts and conduct scenario analysis to assess the potential outcomes of different business decisions. By considering various scenarios and their financial implications, you can anticipate potential challenges, evaluate alternative strategies, and make more informed decisions. Incorporate external factors such as market trends, regulatory changes, and competitive dynamics into your financial forecasts and scenario analysis.

7. Return on Investment (ROI) Analysis: ROI analysis helps entrepreneurs assess the profitability and efficiency of investments or projects. Calculate the ROI by dividing the net profit or gain from the investment by the initial investment cost. Compare the ROI of different projects to prioritize and allocate resources to those with the highest potential returns.

8. Sensitivity Analysis: Sensitivity analysis involves examining how changes in key variables, such as sales volume, costs, or pricing, affect the financial outcomes of a decision. By conducting sensitivity analysis, you can identify the most critical variables and their potential impact on profitability and cash flow. This helps you understand the risks associated with uncertain factors and make more robust financial decisions.

9. Long-Term Financial Planning: Engage in long-term financial planning to ensure the sustainability and growth of your business. Develop financial projections, cash flow forecasts, and budgeting for multiple years. Consider factors such as anticipated revenue growth, capital expenditures, market conditions, and industry trends. Long-term financial planning provides a roadmap for resource allocation, investment decisions, and strategic initiatives.

10. Monitoring and Evaluation: Continuously monitor and evaluate the financial performance of your business. Regularly review financial statements, key performance indicators (KPIs), and benchmarks to assess progress towards financial goals. Implement performance tracking systems and adjust strategies as needed to optimize financial outcomes.

By employing sound financial decision-making principles and strategies, entrepreneurs can make informed choices that enhance the financial health, profitability, and growth of their businesses. Effective financial decision-making ensures that limited resources are allocated wisely, risks are managed effectively, and strategic objectives are achieved.

11.4 Long-Term Financial Planning

Long-term financial planning is a crucial aspect of entrepreneurship that involves setting financial goals, forecasting future financial performance, and developing strategies to achieve sustainable growth and profitability over an extended period. In this section, we will explore the key components and strategies for effective long-term financial planning in the entrepreneurial context.

1. Goal Setting: Begin by defining your long-term financial goals. These goals may include revenue targets, profit margins, market share, return on investment, or any other financial objectives that align with your business's vision and mission. Setting clear and measurable goals provides a framework for your financial planning efforts.

2. Financial Forecasting: Develop financial forecasts that project your business's performance over an extended period, typically three to five years. Forecast your revenues, expenses, and cash flow based on historical data, market trends, industry analysis, and anticipated changes in your business environment. Consider different scenarios and assumptions to account for potential risks and uncertainties.

3. Sales and Revenue Projections: Forecast your future sales and revenue by analyzing market demand, customer trends, competitive dynamics, and marketing strategies. Consider factors such as market size, customer segments, pricing strategies, and potential product or service enhancements. Validate your revenue projections by conducting thorough market research and adjusting them based on market feedback.

4. Expense Budgeting: Develop an expense budget that outlines your projected costs and expenditures over the long term. Consider various cost categories, such as personnel, marketing, operations,

research and development, and administrative expenses. Monitor and control your expenses to ensure they align with your revenue projections and financial goals.

5. Capital Expenditure Planning: Identify the capital expenditures required to support your long-term growth and expansion plans. This may include investments in infrastructure, equipment, technology, or intellectual property. Evaluate the timing and financing options for capital expenditures, considering factors such as cash flow, return on investment, and potential impact on operational efficiency and competitiveness.

6. Risk Assessment and Mitigation: Identify and assess potential financial risks that could impact your long-term financial plan. These risks may include market fluctuations, changes in regulations, technological disruptions, or shifts in customer preferences. Develop strategies to mitigate these risks, such as diversifying revenue streams, maintaining adequate cash reserves, implementing risk management protocols, and staying informed about industry trends and developments.

7. Financing Strategies: Consider your long-term financing needs and develop strategies to secure the necessary capital. Evaluate various financing options, such as equity financing, debt financing, government grants, or strategic partnerships. Assess the costs, terms, and potential impact on ownership and control when selecting the most suitable financing sources.

8. Review and Adjust: Regularly review and update your long-term financial plan to ensure it remains relevant and aligned with your business's evolving needs and external market conditions. Monitor your actual financial performance against the projected figures, identify any variances, and make adjustments as necessary. Stay agile and adaptable to changes in your business environment.

9. Performance Measurement: Establish key performance indicators (KPIs) to track your progress towards your long-term financial goals. Monitor and analyze relevant financial metrics, such as revenue growth, profitability ratios, return on investment, and cash flow generation. Use these metrics to evaluate your business's financial performance, identify areas for improvement, and make informed decisions.

10. Seek Professional Advice: Consider engaging financial professionals, such as accountants, financial advisors, or consultants, to assist you in developing and reviewing your long-term financial plan. Their expertise can provide valuable insights, help validate assumptions, and offer guidance on financial strategies and risk management.

Effective long-term financial planning provides a roadmap for sustainable growth, profitability, and financial stability in your entrepreneurial venture. By setting clear goals, conducting thorough forecasting, implementing sound financial strategies, and regularly reviewing and adjusting your plan, you can navigate the challenges and uncertainties of the business landscape while maximizing your chances of long-term success.

Chapter 12
Leadership and Personal Growth

Introduction

Leadership and personal growth are integral aspects of entrepreneurship that play a vital role in the success and sustainability of your business. As an entrepreneur, you not only need to manage your business but also inspire and lead your team towards achieving common goals. In this section, we will explore the importance of leadership and personal growth in the entrepreneurial journey and provide strategies for developing effective leadership skills and fostering personal growth.

1. The Role of Leadership: Understand the significance of leadership in entrepreneurship. As a leader, you set the vision and direction for your business, inspire and motivate your team, make critical decisions, and create a positive and productive work culture. Effective leadership helps build trust, enhances communication, promotes innovation, and drives the overall success of your venture.

2. Leadership Styles: Explore different leadership styles and identify the one that aligns with your personality, values, and business objectives. Leadership styles can range from autocratic to democratic, transformational to servant leadership. Adapt your leadership style based on the situation, the needs of your team, and the stage of your business's development.

3. Emotional Intelligence: Develop emotional intelligence, which encompasses self-awareness, self-regulation, empathy, and social skills. Emotional intelligence enables you to understand and manage

your emotions effectively, build strong relationships, and navigate interpersonal dynamics. It plays a crucial role in building cohesive and high-performing teams and resolving conflicts constructively.

4. **Effective Communication:** Master the art of effective communication. Clear and transparent communication is essential for sharing the vision and goals of your business, providing feedback, delegating tasks, and fostering a collaborative work environment. Develop active listening skills, use clear and concise language, and adapt your communication style to connect with different team members.

5. **Decision-Making and Problem-Solving:** Enhance your decision-making and problem-solving skills. Entrepreneurship involves making numerous decisions, often under uncertain and complex circumstances. Learn to gather relevant information, analyze alternatives, consider risks and benefits, and make timely and informed decisions. Cultivate a problem-solving mindset that embraces creativity, critical thinking, and adaptability.

6. **Continuous Learning:** Embrace a mindset of continuous learning and personal growth. Stay curious, seek new knowledge, and expand your skill set. Attend industry conferences, participate in workshops, read books and articles, and engage in networking opportunities. Encourage your team members to pursue their own professional development, creating a culture of lifelong learning within your organization.

7. **Building a Support Network:** Surround yourself with a supportive network of mentors, advisors, and like-minded entrepreneurs. Seek guidance from experienced individuals who can provide insights, share their experiences, and offer valuable advice. Engage in entrepreneurship communities and networks to connect with peers, exchange ideas, and learn from their successes and challenges.

8. Work-Life Balance: Strive to maintain a healthy work-life balance. While entrepreneurship often demands long hours and dedication, it's important to prioritize your well-being and personal life. Nurture relationships, engage in hobbies and activities that bring you joy, and take time for self-care. A balanced life enhances your overall effectiveness as a leader and promotes sustainable success.

9. Self-Reflection and Feedback: Engage in regular self-reflection and seek feedback from others. Assess your strengths, weaknesses, and areas for improvement. Embrace constructive feedback as an opportunity for growth and make necessary adjustments to your leadership style and approach. Foster a culture of open feedback within your team, encouraging continuous improvement and learning.

10. Leading by Example: Lead by example and embody the values and behaviors you want to see in your team. Demonstrate integrity, resilience, passion, and a strong work ethic. Be transparent, accountable, and reliable. Your actions and attitudes have a significant impact on your team's morale and motivation.

By investing in your own leadership development and personal growth, you not only enhance your effectiveness as an entrepreneur but also create an environment that nurtures the growth and development of your team. Effective leadership and personal growth are catalysts for building a strong and sustainable business.

12.1 Developing Leadership Skills

Developing leadership skills is a continuous process that involves self-reflection, learning, practice, and adaptation. As an entrepreneur, cultivating effective leadership skills is essential for successfully guiding your business and inspiring your team. In this section, we will explore strategies and practices for developing and enhancing your leadership skills.

1. Self-Awareness: Start by developing self-awareness, which involves understanding your strengths, weaknesses, values, and leadership style. Reflect on your own behaviors, motivations, and decision-making patterns. Assess your emotional intelligence, communication style, and ability to handle stress and pressure. Self-awareness provides the foundation for growth and improvement as a leader.

2. Set Clear Goals: Establish clear goals for your own leadership development. Define the specific leadership skills you want to acquire or improve upon. These goals could include enhancing your communication skills, becoming a better listener, or developing your strategic thinking abilities. Setting clear goals gives you a direction for your learning journey.

3. Seek Learning Opportunities: Actively seek out learning opportunities to expand your leadership skills. Attend workshops, seminars, and conferences focused on leadership and management. Engage in online courses or certifications related to leadership development. Read books and articles written by renowned leaders in your industry. Continuous learning helps you stay updated with the latest trends and best practices in leadership.

4. Find Mentors and Role Models: Identify mentors and role models who can provide guidance and inspiration in your leadership journey.

Seek out individuals who have achieved success in areas that resonate with your aspirations. Connect with them through networking events or professional platforms. Their insights and experiences can provide valuable lessons and perspectives.

5. Practice Active Listening: Develop your active listening skills, which involve giving full attention to others, understanding their perspectives, and responding thoughtfully. Practice empathetic listening, where you genuinely seek to understand the thoughts, feelings, and concerns of your team members. Active listening fosters trust, enhances communication, and strengthens relationships.

6. Build Effective Communication Skills: Effective communication is a cornerstone of leadership. Work on improving your verbal and non-verbal communication skills. Clearly articulate your thoughts, ideas, and expectations. Use appropriate body language and tone of voice to convey your message effectively. Practice active and assertive communication to promote transparency and collaboration.

7. Embrace Feedback: Embrace feedback as a valuable tool for growth and improvement. Encourage your team members to provide constructive feedback on your leadership style, communication, and decision-making. Actively seek feedback from mentors, advisors, or coaches. Reflect on the feedback received and identify areas for refinement. Continuously work on incorporating feedback into your leadership approach.

8. Develop Emotional Intelligence: Emotional intelligence is crucial for effective leadership. Enhance your emotional intelligence by understanding and managing your own emotions as well as recognizing and empathizing with the emotions of others. Cultivate self-regulation, empathy, and social awareness. Emotional intelligence allows you to navigate interpersonal dynamics, resolve conflicts, and build strong relationships.

9. Delegate and Empower: Develop the ability to delegate tasks and empower your team members. Trust in their capabilities and provide them with autonomy to make decisions and take ownership of their work. Effective delegation not only lightens your workload but also fosters a sense of empowerment and accountability among your team.

10. Lead by Example: Lead by example and demonstrate the behaviors and values you expect from your team. Be accountable, honest, and transparent. Show integrity in your actions and decisions. Model a strong work ethic, perseverance, and a commitment to continuous improvement. Leading by example inspires and motivates your team to emulate those qualities.

11. Seek Challenging Opportunities: Seek out challenging opportunities that stretch your leadership skills. Take on projects or roles that require you to develop new skills or lead cross-functional teams. Embrace challenges as opportunities for growth and learning. Stepping out of your comfort zone allows you to develop resilience and adaptability as a leader.

12. Reflect and Adjust: Regularly reflect on your leadership experiences and evaluate your progress. Assess the impact of your leadership style on your team's performance and well-being. Identify areas for improvement and make adjustments as needed. Leadership development is an ongoing process, and being open to learning and adapting is key.

Remember, leadership skills are honed over time through experience, feedback, and a commitment to continuous learning. By investing in your own leadership development, you can create a positive and empowering work environment and effectively guide your business towards success.

12.2 Overcoming Challenges and Failures

Challenges and failures are inevitable parts of the entrepreneurial journey. As a leader, your ability to navigate through these obstacles and learn from failures is crucial for personal growth and the success of your business. In this section, we will explore strategies for overcoming challenges and failures, and turning them into opportunities for growth and resilience.

1. Embrace a Growth Mindset: Adopt a growth mindset, which believes that challenges and failures are opportunities for learning and improvement. Embrace the belief that your abilities and skills can be developed through dedication and hard work. View challenges as chances to grow stronger and failures as stepping stones towards success.

2. Analyze the Situation: When faced with a challenge or failure, take a step back to analyze the situation objectively. Identify the root causes and underlying factors contributing to the problem. Break down the challenge into smaller, manageable tasks or issues that can be addressed effectively.

3. Seek Support: Don't be afraid to seek support from your team, mentors, or advisors. Share your challenges and failures with trusted individuals who can provide guidance and fresh perspectives. Collaborate with your team to brainstorm solutions and leverage their collective knowledge and expertise.

4. Learn from Failure: Instead of dwelling on failures, focus on extracting valuable lessons from them. Reflect on what went wrong, what could have been done differently, and the insights gained from the experience. Use failure as an opportunity to identify areas for improvement and make necessary adjustments to your strategies and approaches.

5. Adapt and Pivot: In the face of challenges, be willing to adapt and pivot your strategies. Evaluate the viability of your current plans and consider alternative approaches. Stay open to new ideas and be flexible in adjusting your course of action. Adaptability is key to overcoming obstacles and finding innovative solutions.

6. Develop Resilience: Cultivate resilience, which is the ability to bounce back from setbacks and maintain a positive mindset. Build your resilience by focusing on the lessons learned from challenges and failures, rather than dwelling on negative emotions. Practice self-care, maintain a support network, and engage in activities that rejuvenate and inspire you.

7. Take Calculated Risks: Entrepreneurship inherently involves taking risks. Evaluate the potential risks and rewards before making decisions. Develop a calculated risk-taking approach by conducting thorough research, analyzing data, and seeking advice. Be willing to step out of your comfort zone and take calculated risks that align with your business goals.

8. Maintain a Long-Term Perspective: Keep a long-term perspective in mind when facing challenges or failures. Understand that setbacks are part of the entrepreneurial journey and that success is often built through perseverance and determination. Focus on your long-term vision and goals, and use challenges as opportunities to learn and grow.

9. Foster a Learning Culture: Create a learning culture within your team and organization. Encourage experimentation, innovation, and continuous improvement. Celebrate and reward efforts and progress, regardless of the outcome. Encourage team members to share their own experiences and insights from challenges and failures, fostering a supportive and collaborative environment.

10. Stay Positive and Motivated: Maintain a positive attitude and stay motivated in the face of challenges. Surround yourself with positive influences and reminders of your vision and goals. Practice gratitude for the progress made and the lessons learned along the way. Your positive energy and resilience will inspire and motivate your team.

Remember, challenges and failures are not indicators of your worth or potential as a leader. They are opportunities for growth, learning, and resilience. By embracing challenges, analyzing failures, and adapting your approach, you can overcome obstacles and lead your team towards success.

12.3 Work-Life Balance and Stress Management

As an entrepreneur, it's easy to get consumed by the demands of running a business, which can lead to imbalances in work and personal life. Achieving a healthy work-life balance and effectively managing stress are essential for your well-being, productivity, and long-term success. In this section, we will explore strategies for maintaining work-life balance and managing stress effectively.

1. Set Priorities: Define your priorities and establish clear boundaries between work and personal life. Identify the most important tasks and responsibilities that require your immediate attention. Delegate tasks that can be handled by others or consider outsourcing certain activities to free up your time and energy.

2. Establish Boundaries: Create boundaries between work and personal life to prevent work from encroaching on your personal time. Set designated work hours and strive to stick to them. Communicate your availability and response time to clients, colleagues, and team members to manage expectations.

3. Delegate and Empower: Delegate tasks to your team members or hire external resources to share the workload. Trust in their capabilities and provide them with the necessary authority to make decisions and take ownership. Effective delegation allows you to focus on strategic initiatives and spend quality time outside of work.

4. Practice Effective Time Management: Implement time management techniques to prioritize tasks and optimize your productivity. Use tools such as to-do lists, calendars, and project management software to stay organized and manage your time efficiently. Break down larger tasks into smaller, manageable segments to prevent overwhelm.

5. Take Breaks and Time Off: Recognize the importance of taking regular breaks throughout the workday to recharge and refocus. Step away from your workspace, engage in activities that relax and rejuvenate you, and return with a fresh perspective. Additionally, make it a priority to take time off for vacations and personal commitments to restore balance and prevent burnout.

6. Nurture Supportive Relationships: Cultivate supportive relationships with family, friends, and mentors who understand and support your entrepreneurial journey. Share your challenges, seek their advice, and lean on them for emotional support. Strong personal relationships provide a sense of stability and help you maintain perspective amidst the demands of work.

7. Practice Self-Care: Prioritize self-care activities that promote physical, mental, and emotional well-being. Engage in regular exercise, eat a balanced diet, get enough sleep, and incorporate stress-reduction techniques such as meditation or mindfulness practices into your routine. Taking care of your well-being enhances your ability to handle stress and maintain work-life balance.

8. Learn to Say No: It's important to set boundaries and learn to say no to commitments or requests that don't align with your priorities or values. Overcommitting yourself can lead to increased stress and diminished quality of work. Evaluate opportunities and obligations carefully before accepting them.

9. Seek Support: Don't hesitate to seek support from mentors, business coaches, or support groups specifically for entrepreneurs. Surround yourself with individuals who understand the unique challenges you face and can offer guidance and perspective. Sharing experiences and challenges with like-minded individuals can alleviate stress and provide valuable insights.

10. Regularly Evaluate and Adjust: Regularly assess your work-life balance and stress levels. Reflect on what's working and what needs adjustment. Be proactive in identifying areas where improvements can be made and implement necessary changes. Work-life balance is a continuous journey that requires ongoing evaluation and adjustment.

Remember, achieving work-life balance and managing stress is an ongoing process. It's important to be patient with yourself and allow for flexibility as you navigate the demands of entrepreneurship. By prioritizing self-care, setting boundaries, and seeking support, you can create a more fulfilling and sustainable entrepreneurial journey.

12.4 Continuous Learning and Professional Development

In the fast-paced world of entrepreneurship, continuous learning and professional development are vital for staying ahead of the curve, adapting to changes, and fostering personal growth. As a leader, it is important to invest in your own learning journey and encourage a culture of learning within your organization. In this section, we will explore strategies for continuous learning and professional development.

1. Embrace a Growth Mindset: Adopt a growth mindset that emphasizes the belief that abilities and intelligence can be developed through dedication and hard work. Embrace challenges, view setbacks as opportunities for learning, and maintain a curiosity to explore new ideas and perspectives.

2. Seek Knowledge and Resources: Stay updated with industry trends, market developments, and best practices through various sources of knowledge. Read books, articles, and research papers related to your industry. Follow influential thought leaders and experts in your field. Attend conferences, workshops, and seminars to gain insights and network with like-minded professionals.

3. Expand Your Skill Set: Identify the skills that are essential for your role as an entrepreneur and continually work on developing them. This could include areas such as leadership, communication, negotiation, financial management, marketing, or technology. Take advantage of online courses, webinars, and workshops to enhance your skills and stay current with industry advancements.

4. Networking and Collaboration: Build a strong professional network by actively engaging with industry peers, mentors, and experts. Attend networking events, join professional associations, and participate in online communities. Collaborate with others on projects or initiatives that provide opportunities for mutual learning and growth.

5. Mentorship and Coaching: Seek guidance and mentorship from experienced entrepreneurs or business professionals who can provide valuable insights and support. Consider engaging a business coach or mentor who can offer personalized guidance tailored to your specific needs and challenges.

6. Experiment and Learn from Failure: Embrace a culture of experimentation within your organization and encourage your team members to take calculated risks. Celebrate both successes and failures as opportunities for learning and growth. Analyze failures to understand the underlying causes and identify lessons that can be applied to future endeavors.

7. Foster a Learning Culture: Create an environment that values and promotes continuous learning. Encourage your team members to pursue professional development opportunities and provide resources and support to facilitate their growth. Implement regular knowledge-sharing sessions, where individuals can share their expertise and learn from one another.

8. Stay Informed about Technology and Innovation: Keep abreast of technological advancements and emerging trends relevant to your industry. Leverage technology to streamline processes, enhance productivity, and gain a competitive edge. Stay connected with the startup ecosystem and explore opportunities for collaboration or partnerships with innovative companies.

9. Reflect and Evaluate: Regularly take time to reflect on your experiences, successes, and challenges. Evaluate the outcomes of your initiatives and projects. Identify areas for improvement and develop action plans for personal and professional growth. Solicit feedback from trusted sources and use it to enhance your skills and performance.

10. Lead by Example: As a leader, demonstrate a commitment to continuous learning and professional development. Share your learning experiences, insights, and recommended resources with your team. Encourage and support their individual learning journeys, and create opportunities for them to grow and take on new challenges.

Remember, continuous learning and professional development are ongoing processes that require dedication and commitment. By embracing a growth mindset, seeking knowledge, expanding your skill set, and fostering a learning culture, you can continuously evolve as an entrepreneur and drive the growth and success of your business.

Conclusion

In conclusion, entrepreneurship is a journey that begins with a dream and requires dedication, resilience, and the right mindset to turn that dream into reality. Throughout this book, we have explored the essential aspects of entrepreneurship, from identifying opportunities and creating a business plan to building a strong foundation, securing funding, and developing effective marketing and sales strategies. We have also delved into the importance of leadership, adaptability, financial management, and continuous learning.

Entrepreneurship is not without its challenges. It requires a willingness to take risks, face uncertainties, and overcome obstacles along the way. However, with the right knowledge, skills, and mindset, aspiring entrepreneurs can navigate these challenges and increase their chances of success.

The entrepreneurial mindset is a critical foundation for any aspiring entrepreneur. It involves developing the characteristics of successful entrepreneurs, such as passion, resilience, creativity, and a strong work ethic. By cultivating an entrepreneurial mindset, individuals can approach problems as opportunities, embrace innovation and change, and persist in the face of adversity.

Identifying opportunities is a crucial step in the entrepreneurial journey. It involves recognizing market gaps and trends, conducting market research, and assessing personal interests and skills. By identifying viable business opportunities, entrepreneurs can capitalize on emerging trends and meet the needs of target customers.

Creating a comprehensive business plan is essential for guiding the entrepreneurial journey. A business plan outlines the vision, mission, goals, and strategies of the venture. It also includes components such as the value proposition, competitive analysis, financial projections, and budgeting. A well-crafted business plan provides a roadmap for entrepreneurs and serves as a communication tool when seeking funding or partnerships.

Building a strong foundation involves selecting the right legal structure, registering the business, understanding intellectual property rights, and setting up a professional network. These foundational elements lay the groundwork for a sustainable and legally compliant business operation.

Funding is a critical aspect of entrepreneurship, and entrepreneurs must explore different funding options, understand the pros and cons of bootstrapping versus external financing, and learn how to craft an effective pitch deck to attract investors or secure loans.

Building a winning team is essential for entrepreneurial success. Hiring the right people, creating a company culture, practicing effective team management, and motivating and retaining employees are all crucial elements in building a high-performing and cohesive team.

Developing a robust marketing strategy is vital for reaching target customers and achieving business growth. This involves defining the target market, branding and positioning the business, implementing digital marketing strategies, and measuring and adjusting marketing efforts based on data and analytics.

Sales and customer acquisition play a crucial role in driving revenue and business growth. Building a sales pipeline, employing effective sales techniques, implementing customer relationship management strategies, and scaling sales operations are essential for success in this area.

Scaling and expansion are key considerations as the business grows. Entrepreneurs need to develop strategies for growth, scale operations and production, enter new markets, and manage risk and sustainability to ensure long-term success and profitability.

Innovation and adaptability are critical for staying ahead of the competition and thriving in a rapidly changing business landscape. Entrepreneurs must embrace change and disruption, foster innovation within their business, adapt to industry trends, and continuously strive to stay ahead of their competitors.

Financial management and planning are vital for the sustainability and profitability of the business. Understanding financial statements, budgeting and cash flow management, financial decision-making, and long-term financial planning are essential skills for entrepreneurs to master.

Leadership and personal growth are intertwined with entrepreneurial success. Developing leadership skills, overcoming challenges and failures, maintaining work-life balance and managing stress, and engaging in continuous learning and professional development are all crucial for personal and professional growth as an entrepreneur.

As we reach the end of this book, I hope that it has provided you with valuable insights, practical strategies, and a solid foundation to embark on your entrepreneurial journey.

 Remember that entrepreneurship requires dedication, perseverance, and continuous learning. Embrace the challenges, stay adaptable, and remain passionate about your vision. With the right mindset and knowledge, you have the power to transform your dreams into reality. Good luck on your entrepreneurial path!

Dear readers,

I want to express my gratitude for joining me on this journey through the pages of "Entrepreneurship : From Dream to Reality." It has been a privilege to share my knowledge and insights with you, and I hope that this book has provided you with valuable guidance and inspiration as you embark on your own entrepreneurial endeavors.

Remember, entrepreneurship is not just about starting a business—it's a mindset, a way of thinking, and a commitment to continuous growth and innovation. Embrace the challenges, learn from failures, and celebrate successes along the way. Surround yourself with a supportive network, seek knowledge, and never stop learning.

Always believe in yourself and your vision. Your dreams can become a reality if you have the passion, perseverance, and determination to make them happen. Stay focused, adaptable, and open to new opportunities. Trust your instincts and be willing to take calculated risks.

Lastly, remember that entrepreneurship is not a solo journey. Collaborate with others, seek guidance from mentors, and build a strong team around you. Together, you can achieve great things and make a positive impact in the world.

Thank you once again for joining me on this exciting adventure. I wish you all the best in your entrepreneurial pursuits. May you find fulfillment, success, and personal growth on your path to turning your dreams into reality.

Best regards,
-Sagar Shinde